Everybody Loves Oprah!

Everybody Loves OPRAH!

Her Remarkable Life Story

Norman King

Quill
William Morrow
New York

Library of Congress Cataloging-in-Publication Data

King, Norman, 1926–
Everybody loves Oprah! : her remarkable life story / Norman King.
p. cm.
Bibliography: p.
ISBN 0-688-07950-4 (pbk.)
1. Winfrey, Oprah. 2. Television personalities—United States—Biography. 3. Motion picture actors and actresses—United States—Biography. I. Title.
PN1992.4.W56K5 1988
791.45'092'4—dc19
[B] 88-333
CIP

Printed in the United States of America

First Quill Edition

1 2 3 4 5 6 7 8 9 10

BOOK DESIGN BY ANN GOLD

Contents

Everybody Loves Oprah!

1
The Main Event

In this corner . . . Oprah Winfrey!

To experience Oprah Winfrey for the first time, you are aware, immediately, of a sense of almost pervasive human warmth, an enveloping hug of empathy, compassion, and trustworthiness.

And only then are you able to focus on the smiling, welcoming, beautiful face—surrounded by that distinguishing halo of luxuriant black hair.

It is the *eyes* that are overpowering—eyes the size of residential swimming pools, as one admirer has put it.

Behind the eyes, as you continue to gaze, you can see glimpses of an original intelligence that peeps through on occasion to reveal the presence of the remarkable woman within.

Then of course your eyes see the huge bouncing earrings, the fingers clutching the portable microphone in the jeweled fist, and the bright-colored scarf tossed casually over the expensively tailored designer gown made especially for her.

And that—seen and engraved on the mind in a split second—is the phenomenon called Oprah Gail Winfrey.

But the first split-second glimpse never tells the full story of anyone. For this woman, who is passionately interested in dieting and in studying men, is also as passionately interested in rape victims, in victims of child molestation, and even in members of racist groups pitted against all people of her own black race.

Unpredictable. This is the key word for Oprah Winfrey, the Chicago talk-show hostess who at the age of thirty arrived in Chicago to take over an ailing morning show and since that moment has steered it quickly and assertively into the stratosphere, where it has outrated Phil Donahue, the acknowledged king of the talk-show business.

You can never be sure where Oprah is coming from. She is a kaleidoscope of contrasting attributes—feminine one moment, brassy the next, earthy soon after, soulful immediately following that, tasteless and taunting anytime, and then . . . sassy.

"When you tune in the station she is on, you take your chances," one might say of her. "But you always get a good show!"

One moment she will be discussing the value of penis size in relation to feminine satisfaction in sexual intercourse, the next she will be talking about the study of sixteenth-century literature.

Television columnist Howard Rosenberg described her in this fashion:

"She's a roundhouse, a full-course meal, big, brassy, loud, aggressive, hyper, laughable, lovable, soulful, tender, low-down, earthy, and hungry. And she may know the way to Phil Donahue's jugular."

Yes. That is Oprah Winfrey—in this corner.

And in *this* corner . . . Phil Donahue!

Everybody knows Phil Donahue. He's the talk-show host with the biggest following any person in daytime television has ever had. He is the man whose skin Oprah

Winfrey is after. She's coming to get him—and on his very own turf!

Is this match a fantasy, or the real thing? That was what had everybody wondering in the fall of 1986.

And, yes, it was indeed the real thing—an honest-to-God battle scheduled to take place during the week of September 8, the opening of the 1986 fall television season. It would pit the challenger—Oprah Winfrey—against the champion—Phil Donahue—during a week in which the newcomer was mounting a new syndicated talk show against Donahue's firmly entrenched show . . . *on a national scale.*

Oh?

"Donahue's entertaining, often stimulating, long-running show is still a national champ," said Rosenberg. "Yet Oprah trounced him in the Chicago ratings, earning this much-publicized coast-to-coast shot for the versatile Winfrey."

More was at stake in this duel than simply a popularity contest between two personable celebrity types. Much more.

Although, of course, the individuals were interesting in themselves—as interesting as any two contenders would be in any contest of this magnitude—each, in fact, differed from the other about as much as could be possible, even in the varied and multiethnic United States of America.

The reigning champion was a white male, born in 1935, from a solid middle-class background, had been raised a Catholic, had married, divorced, and married again.

The challenger was a black female, born out of wedlock in 1954, into an impoverished farm family, was sexually abused as a child, was raised a Protestant, and was unmarried.

Yet in spite of these disparities, there were surprising similarities between these two contenders—peculiar talents that helped to make each a best in this strange breed of broadcast celebrities, the talk-show proprietor.

- Each nourished a desire from childhood to be a dramatic artist on the stage or on the screen.
- Each was sharp, mentally alert, quick, and dedicated to reading and studying.
- Each projected an amazing aura of charisma whenever he or she appeared in public.

As if those similarities might not be enough, each of the contenders began his or her career as a reporter, later reading the news on radio and television and anchoring television newscasts in various cities.

What might be the most important thing of all, however, was the fact that each of these contenders was born and raised in an area of the country termed by the majority of the population as the "boondocks." Neither came from the more intellectually oriented East or West Coast. Nor did either, although they were both college graduates, have an Ivy League education.

What was more to the point, both made the breakthrough to the big time in one specific city—Chicago, Illinois. Not Los Angeles, not San Francisco, not Boston, not New York. Chicago—the second-largest city in the United States.

But all this was simply part of the contrast that was making this contest such a lively and exciting one. First of all, the *stakes* were what mattered the most.

The *stakes.*

Yes. It was the money that was on the line in this contest—the huge amounts being put up by each side to make sure that its contender would win the ratings game.

Donahue himself—the champ—had first mined the fertile daytime hours of television broadcasting with his pioneering talk-show formula. Up to the time he began to substitute controversy for cooking recipes, the revenue from shows on television in the daylight hours came mostly from the network soap operas—continuations of the old-fashioned tearjerkers of an earlier era.

These shows were network attractions—not syndicated offerings. But there were a lot of independent stations out there that needed competition to slot against the network offerings. These stations could produce their own live shows—highly unlikely in view of the expense—or they could purchase syndicated offerings. Syndication usually involved repeats of popular prime-time shows; but original show ideas were now being produced for national syndication every day.

And it was here that Donahue began to pull the viewers—and thus revenue—away from the three major networks, at first in a small way, and then later in a very big way. Some of the network shows even bought him in syndication to keep him from taking away viewers! If you can't beat 'em, join 'em!

The figures tell the story. In 1975, for example, when Donahue had been going just a little over seven years, the total of nonnetwork television advertising revenue added up to $263 million a year. Ten years later, in 1985, that figure was up around $990 million. As for the total figures for daytime television—both network and nonnetwork—1975 generated $820 million, and 1985 $2.56 billion. Up three times!

Because of his success, the independents were shopping around for shows that had the Donahue magic. They were hard to find. Donahue had put his imprint on the formula and made it almost exclusively his own.

With the revenues from syndicated daytime shows approaching the billion-dollar mark annually, it was obvious that daytime television was big-time stuff!

It was also known throughout the industry that many of the stations purchasing the *Donahue* show were using it to anchor their daytime schedules, figuring that if one watched *Donahue*, the chances were that one might continue watching whatever followed *Donahue*.

"The viewers he draws to a channel," one programmer said, "often stay there for hours."

And those were the stakes in the coming bout between Oprah Winfrey and Phil Donahue—the battle that might determine the occupation of the daytime television battleground for decades to come!

The Oprah-Donahue confrontation actually had begun in 1984, when the challenger arrived in Chicago from Baltimore. This was during the last year that Donahue was broadcasting from Chicago, just before his move to New York early in 1985.

Oprah, who had come in from the South to appear opposite him in the early months of 1984, suddenly began to run the man ragged, almost displacing him in his own comfortable 9 A.M. slot!

Who the hell was this Oprah Winfrey? The horrible truth was that she was using the same talk-show format that he himself had *invented*. Okay, then—*perfected*. Nevertheless . . .

When Oprah *immediately* surged ahead of the king of the format in the Chicago area, people began to sit up and take notice. Especially the people who controlled the money allotted for daytime television programming.

Oprah's show remained local for a year and a half, but then it was expanded from a half hour to an hour; later it was renamed—from the prosaic *A.M. Chicago* to the more personal *Oprah Winfrey Show*.

It was at this point that King World, the whoppingly successful syndicator of hit shows like *Wheel of Fortune,* decided to take on Oprah Winfrey and play her nationally in the same areas where the Donahue show was safely ensconced.

The date of her national debut was set, and the duel

was to be the squaring off of the challenger against the established champion.

The card was set:

Event
Knockdown bout, no holds barred

Reigning Champion
Phil Donahue

Challenger
Oprah Winfrey

Time
The week of September 8, 1986

Place
National television

Purse
Open-ended, to be determined by syndication numbers

That was the card.

To foment interest in their client, King World began issuing challenges to Multimedia Entertainment, the syndicators of the fabulously successful *Donahue* show. The challenge was the inevitable question: Who is better—Donahue or Oprah? It became a Donahue vs. Oprah contest. Strategically, this was sound publicity practice, establishing Oprah's image in the minds of those who had never heard of her. Many of these challenges were in the form of statements attributed to Oprah herself.

"People have the power to make a difference in their lives," she said, referring to the fact that her show tackled such provocative subjects as sex, divorce, battered women, rape, and incest. Well, so did Donahue's, of course. He had *pioneered* the use of these subjects. Anyway—

"We want to let people know that," she went on. "That's the beauty of good television. Good television should inform and inspire as well as entertain. So much of television is simply mindless." Mindless = *Donahue*? So it had been said somewhere. . . .

The champion's camp came back with the expected rejoinder: "That's a challenging thing," Donahue told an interviewer when questioned as to how he felt about Oprah Winfrey going up against him in at least one out of four of his key cities.

"We're on a more competitive street now than we've been on. We're up. We're fascinated by the attention that's been generated. We think it's good for the daytime schedule." Not really an answer to the question, was it?

And Oprah Winfrey even had something gracious to say about the format. "Without Donahue [my] show wouldn't be possible. He showed that women have an interest in things that affect their lives and not just how to stuff cabbage. Because of that I have nothing to prove, only to do good shows. . . . I say, he's the king and I just want a little piece of the kingdom."

Then Stuart Hersch, chief operating officer of King World, got in a word:

"We're not out to wipe Donahue off the face of the earth, but it's plausible we'll knock him off the air."

"Hype," riposted the Donahue camp. The victory of the Oprah Winfrey show in Chicago was probably a fluke that would not translate into nationwide success, they said.

"They're building a whole piece of cloth out of one little thread," said Janet Baser, vice-president of research at Multimedia.

But the image makers around Oprah continued to push her as a cocky and feisty hostess with "grand plans to unseat Donahue as America's favorite daytime talk-show host."

To which Multimedia's Baser responded: "She'll have

to come out of the box and do very good numbers to match the hype." Translation: Oprah will have to emerge from the publicity package in which she has been wrapped and attract many new viewers to merit the excessive press raves about her.

Actually, even King World knew how fraught with danger the challenge was for Oprah. If she could knock Donahue flat, of course she would be considered the winner. If she could equal Donahue, she could also be considered successful.

But if she surged ahead fast, riding the crest of public curiosity over the question "Who is this Oprah Winfrey?" and then leveled off later on to fall below Donahue's established level, she would be dead in the water. What was more to the point, such a surge and fall would mean eventually that she would sink even further in the months following, until in the long run she might be totally out of sight in a national sense.

The choices were narrowed now almost to nothing. She *must* win, and win big, *and* continue to pull in more viewers than the old master. Otherwise she would prove to be exactly what her detractors were making her out to be—a flash in the pan.

No wonder she said about national syndication, "I've got *hives* just thinking about it!"

By the time the bout was slated to begin, she had 128 stations safely tucked away in her bag. Exuding confidence, she charmed most of her buyers with her boisterous, sassy, and brassy manner.

Tucked away, yes—temporarily. But of course all those contracts had escape clauses in them. If Oprah did not pull hard and continue to pull hard, they could always be canceled out.

The battle began—right on schedule.

Oprah Winfrey was hoping to make the difference through sheer force of personality and talent. While less articulate, intellectual, and polished than Donahue, she was more explosive and unpredictable.

Donahue himself, the dominant performer, and with no distaste for introducing gratuitously titillating topics where ratings were concerned, hoped to win on the fact that his show imparted information as well as excitement.

Round One
Monday

All week before the fateful Monday, the Oprah Winfrey camp had remained silent about what it would air for her initial offering on national television. Speculation was, as they say, "rife" among members of the broadcast reviewing community. The obvious thing was for her to guest-star a personality of unquestionable magnitude and interest. Maybe Steven Spielberg would drop by; he had put her in the public eye by casting her for a key role in his movie *The Color Purple*. Or perhaps Quincy Jones, the man on Spielberg's team who had actually discovered Oprah Winfrey there in Chicago on her talk show. Or maybe Michael Jackson, who thought sometimes the same way Oprah did—and at other times emphatically did *not*.

Big stuff?

Or would she go to her main strength, which was the discussion in a low-key way of the basic problems of the people in her audience? Sex? Marriage? Careers? Or some other "everyday" problem with which she was so well equipped to deal?

And so it finally came.

The selection was, in truth, not exactly on the strong side or meaningful in itself. It turned out to be an examination of what it takes to snare a mate in the cutthroat world of the 1980s—a kind of spinoff of the Helen Gurley Brown–*Cosmopolitan* basic motif.

"How many guys here have slept with a girl on the first date?" Oprah asked her audience on Monday.

(Howard Rosenberg noted in the *Los Angeles Times:* "It was that kind of show in that kind of week." Bill Carter, of the *Baltimore Sun,* put it this way: "With a topic like mate-catching, Winfrey could wing it in high style.")

And did she ever wing it—jumping back and forth from her "guest star" to people who had purchased the guest star's books on catching a mate. This woman had written two books that cost $95 apiece—that is not a typographical error: $95 apiece!

Well, anyway—these two "guide" books *did* have a money-back guarantee—"If you can find her," Oprah observed at one point.

Actually, people who had read the books and acted on them gave both positive and negative responses. There were even brief street interviews with people at the beginning of each segment featuring related questions—questions such as, "On what date should you first go to bed with your date?" "How soon is too soon?" The conclusion? "Wait till the third date." Then, obviously—Geronimo!

Oprah was funny at times, and at others blunt. One male in the audience explained how much better he was now at dating. He attributed it to the fact that he was using the book's suggestions that he display more self-confidence.

Oprah turned to him with that beaming, high-voltage smile. "So you're saying you were a wimp before?"

She also turned her sense of humor against her guest, deflating that woman's ego just a bit. The book, Oprah said, had this bit of fundamental advice in it:

"If you have to belch at a dinner party, do it privately." The star stood there stupefied, staring at the book. Oprah went on: "Who wouldn't know *that* already?"

The guide even discussed how much jewelry should be

worn. Its author gratuitously noted, on the air, that Oprah was wearing the wrong kind of earrings. A bit testily, Oprah asked what was wrong with them. After all, she *always* wore earrings; she *loved* them; they were part of her.

"They get in the way of kissing your earlobes," the author explained.

Oprah shrugged and glowered. "They can kiss my kneecaps."

Somehow, Oprah Winfrey seemed to keep it all together, particularly by her ingenuity and her ability to inject generous helpings of Oprah Winfrey *herself* in the show to keep it alive and bubbling.

She also set up several laughs in the skillful way she handled the subject. Some of the comments seemed to be scripted in advance—especially those of the "author," who displayed that very professional and slick manner that talk-show types usually have, with a brimful repertoire of one-liners memorized and ready for instant extraction from the mind-file.

The show itself? How did the critics react?

"A fluff ball of a subject," Bill Carter wrote, "that probably went over extremely well with the normal morning television audience. The show itself was unstintingly forgettable, but the star wasn't."

"For some reason, she comes over more sincere than Donahue," *Newsday* said. "I know you won't believe this. Phil majored in sincerity in college. He set the standards for sincerity by which everybody is judged. Oprah out-sinceres Phil."

As for Donahue himself—he entered the ring with a show on the "Mayflower Madam." Sydney Biddle Barrows, the ambitious member of a socially prominent New York family, two of whose ancestors had sailed on the *Mayflower,* was the tabloid sensation of 1985 when she was found guilty of running three very high-class call-girl rings that listed as Johns many prominent Manhattan businessmen. The interview with Barrows, the author of *Mayflower Madam,* which was a detailed story about her enterprise, was typical Donahue—well sculptured, and nicely received by the friendly and expectant audience always properly titillated by the sexual peccadilloes of old-line blue bloods.

Who led in the first round?

"[Oprah Winfrey] brings expansive energy and spontaneous enthusiasm to this tired format, while leaving out the psycho-intellectual bilge that has turned the previous talk-show giant, Phil Donahue, into a pretentious bore," wrote Bill Carter.

Round Two
Tuesday

Oprah came out swinging, this time with a show titled "Feuding Families." The idea was a solid one. There were three groups of feuders who appeared on the guest panel.

GROUP ONE: Two white sisters who were no longer speaking to one another because one had told their mother that the other was dating a black man.

The second sister was no longer speaking to the tattletale sister, and the tattletale had decided not to speak to her victim either.

GROUP TWO: Two black sisters who were no longer speaking to one another because one owed the other $50 and had not returned two wine glasses she had borrowed.

The accusing sister noted, "She knows how I feel about my wine glasses!"

GROUP THREE: A mother-daughter combo. They were no longer speaking to each other because the mother had not attended her daughter's wedding. Nor did she even approve of the marriage.

The daughter's husband was in the audience. He rose

and confronted the mother. They came out swinging at one another. Verbally.

A fitting climax to the show? Perfect! Except that it wasn't the finale. It was only the first half!

The last half hour involved a rabbi therapist who specialized in feuding families. There were other feuding members of families in the audience, and these rose one by one to give their own testimony about personal feuds.

After a station break, Oprah Winfrey revealed that two of the feuding family members in the audience had made up right there during the commercial.

This was all very touching, one critic noted. One wondered, he went on, how all these people who could not stand one another had been tricked or inveigled into appearing on the show together. Or were they enticed some other way? And if not, why had they decided to come?

Also, where had the staff of the show found these people? Were there halfway houses for feuding family members? Was there a school for them?

At the end of the show, the two white sisters still were unable to communicate with one another; the two black sisters could not get together either. Nor would the mother-daughter team speak to one another.

Failure! Abject failure.

And Donahue?

To counteract Oprah's "Feuding Families," he did an hour on "Baby Jesse" with the child's parents. This was blockbuster programming. Baby Jesse, born with hypoplastic heart syndrome—a fatal malady—had received a heart transplant when only sixteen days old, but only after first being refused the operation because his parents, Jesse Dean Sepulveda and Deana Binkley, were not married. It was in fact the appearance of Sepulveda and Binkley on the *Donahue* show of June 10, 1986, that made the hospital in Loma Linda, California, rethink its priorities and secure a heart donor for Baby Jesse. Donahue obviously intended to remind his viewers that he had helped save the boy's life.

Round Three Wednesday

This turned out to be a favorite subject of Oprah Winfrey's: "People of the Aryan Nations." "PAN" was a group of white supremacists whose leaders admitted that they had ties to the Nazis and to the Ku Klux Klan. Obviously, they were excited about getting such extremely wide-ranging prime-time television exposure for their clanking ideologies.

Oprah opened it up by getting them to talk about how they hated all non-Aryans, especially Jewish people. They said that they believed the Jews definitely wanted to mix all races together, to "mongrelize" the world.

Keeping her cool, Oprah bore down on the racist members of the panel, simply asking them to express their point of view. But it was not to be a simple declaration of their beliefs.

In the middle of the show Oprah introduced Peter Lake, a reporter who had gone undercover in the organization to take pictures of the PAN groups in operation. Lake accused the members of the Aryan Nations of violent acts, including murder.

Later Judd Rose, an ABC newscaster, was introduced by the star. He showed footage ABC-TV had had on file, showing a member of Aryan Nations taking target practice. The target at which the members were shooting was a blown-up photograph of former Israeli prime minister Menachem Begin.

Oprah's comment was memorable—and just a bit sassy in itself: "He ain't got no hook nose no more."

At this point, the show almost broke up, with the invited guests charging that the pictures were untrue—"out of context," and so on. Members of the audience got up and expressed their views—some against the Aryan Nations, and some in favor.

At the end of the hour, Oprah Winfrey was draping her arm over the shoulder of a man in the audience who was sympathetic to the white supremacists on the panel.

Tawney Little, a newscaster in Los Angeles, later interviewed David Lehrer of the Anti-Defamation League about the show. "You have to be thrilled about a show like Oprah's today," she suggested.

Lehrer had reservations. He was not exactly thrilled by it. But, he admitted, at least her program provided more rebuttal to the group than an earlier episode broadcast on the *Donahue* show, which had provided a similar platform for the white-supremacist Posse Comitatus.

LITTLE: Did Winfrey err in putting the Aryan Nations on television?

LEHRER: It was a close call.

Columnist Howard Rosenberg of the *Los Angeles Times* disagreed; it was *not* a close call at all: "It's an *easy* call. No free air time. When racists are legitimate news, cover them. When they're propagandizing, ignore them. The issue is not free speech, but free air time. The Aryan Nations wasn't making news Wednesday. It was making rating points for *Oprah Winfrey*. In doing so it was getting a crack at a national television audience and, while exposing itself to ridicule, also gaining a measure of respectability by being associated with an established television host. And a black one, to boot."

Rosenberg summed up the situation in this fashion: "It was good television, all right, but was it wise television?"

Donahue's riposte? "Divorced Couples Face Off."

Round Four
Thursday

Oprah came out of the corner with "Women Molested and Raped by Their Doctors."

Donahue did "Designer Drugs," interviewing a number of physicians and scientists.

By this time, to all intents and purposes, the battle was pretty much over. And the ratings for the first three days were conclusive—at least in the Los Angeles area, which was the most important and critical one because it was a *first*—and thus a key harbinger of the future—for Oprah Winfrey.

Donahue won Monday with a 26 percent audience share, to a 23 percent for Winfrey. But Winfrey clobbered him on Tuesday, 30 percent to 18 percent, and won again on Wednesday, with a 29 percent to 22 percent share.

The reviewers now began coming out of their corners, however, with estimates of each contender's worth.

"She may be an inch deep," wrote Steve Daley, a *Chicago Tribune* columnist, "but she's irresistible."

"In Donahue, the veteran, and Winfrey, the newly arrived," Les Payne wrote in *Newsday*, "we have two masters of the con. In bowing their audience's strings, they make full use of the fact that they are not white women. Both are skilled actors, each knows when to caress a wrist or touch a shoulder or milk an emotion just so."

He added, "Oprah Winfrey is sharper than Donahue, wittier, more genuine and far better attuned to her audience, if not the world."

But the problem, according to Payne, was "that Winfrey's role, at bottom, is to play the reassuring Black Nanny to her dominant white female audience."

Also: "Others have criticized Winfrey for not employing

enough black staffers and citing performance 'excellence' as the reason."

Another reviewer, Martha Bayles of *The Wall Street Journal,* wrote: "Mr. Donahue's real talent is for eliciting and dramatizing other people's points of view, not for propagating his own. I mean, how brightly can a dim bulb shine? As for Ms. Winfrey, she exudes neither light nor heat, but warmth. Where Phil drops bombs, Oprah spreads balm."

And so, "Ms. Winfrey's message is nothing new on the American scene: the power of positive thinking, with a little faddish spirituality tossed in. She certainly doesn't preach like a traditional Baptist. But after years of watching Mr. Donahue sweat and strain to remind the world that he is no longer a parochial-minded Irish Catholic, it's a relief to see a gabmonger with a fond but realistic assessment of her own cultural and religious roots. Understanding both the good and bad about her background enables Ms. Winfrey to suffer fools a little less glibly."

Obviously, Oprah was the winner in this battle of the talk-show proprietors—at least in the first head-to-head contest on a national scale.

Who was this person who could take on the giant on his own turf and bring back his scalp within such a short time? Who was she and how had she gotten where she was so quickly?

And why did everybody seem to love Oprah—so *soon*?

2
Life with Grandmother

Oprah Winfrey was born on February 1, 1954, in a tiny Southern town with the somewhat unlikely name of Kosciusko, Mississippi. Upon further examination, however, the name—derived from a Polish war hero of the American Revolution named Thaddeus Kosciusko—does not seem quite so unlikely.

In those parts of the South the word *rebel* even today has a heroic ring to it—and somehow Oprah grew up in that same tradition of rebellion, which she has never really given up. The town, incidentally, is located about seventy miles north of Jackson, the largest city in the state, named after another somewhat rebellious spitfire, Andrew Jackson.

Her parents were as rebellious as Oprah proved to be—rebels against the social status quo in which they lived. At the time of their daughter's birth they were unmarried, and separated by some 250 miles—her mother in Kosciusko, and her father at Fort Rucker, where he was stationed in the armed services. Shortly after the birth of her daughter, the mother left town and headed for Milwaukee, Wisconsin, without her.

In fact, Oprah herself attributes her conception to what she calls "a one-day fling under an oak tree." She, the offspring that resulted, was as unexpected as the "fling" that produced her. Her father and mother, Oprah says, never repeated their union after that first time.

Her father, twenty years old at her birth, was Vernon Winfrey, who later moved to Nashville, Tennessee, and became a barber, a grocer, an elected councilman, and a deacon in the Baptist church, but was not doing much of anything around Kosciusko at the time except being in uniform in the service of his country.

Her mother, Vernita Lee, was eighteen years old and a farm girl, and was ready any day to split Kosciusko and go north, where there was more work and more money to be made.

"I am not proud of what happened with Oprah's mother and me," Vernon Winfrey said many years later about the incident of Oprah's birth. "I tell people today that if something like that happens, the boy should help take care of the child."

Vernon, however, did not. Stationed at Camp Rucker in the wilds of Alabama, he did not even know that Vernita was pregnant. He went back to the base after spending his leave at home in Kosciusko and, in terms of Vernita at least, it was a case of "out of sight, out of mind."

Obviously, there was an ironic similarity between the given names of Oprah Winfrey's two parents—Vernon and Vernita. It is just one of those small details that make Oprah Winfrey's origins at once interesting, fated-to-be, and somehow just a bit make-believe unbelievable.

Also unbelievable is the fact that *Oprah* is not really the name her mother intended to give to her at all, but a spoonerism that occurred accidentally somewhere between her birth in Vernita Lee's house and the filing of the birth certificate in Kosciusko.

Actually, it was a sister of Vernita's who suggested her

daughter be named *Orpah,* a biblical name from the Book of Ruth in the Old Testament. As any student of the Bible knows, Orpah was the sister-in-law of Ruth. When the two sons of Bethlehem-born Naomi died in Moab—what is now known as Jordan—Naomi called together their wives and bade them farewell; she was going to return to Bethlehem. She suggested that her daughters-in-law go their own way—that is, stay in Moab with their families. The Bible goes on with the story:

> And they lifted up their voice, and wept again: and Orpah kissed her mother in law; but Ruth clave unto her.

It was then that Ruth told Naomi that she would return with her to Bethlehem, and in explanation, uttered what may be some of the most famous lines in the Bible:

> For whither thou goest, I will go; and where thou lodgest, I will lodge: thy people *shall be* my people, and thy God my God: where thou diest, will I die, and there will I be buried.

Orpah stayed in Moab, and disappeared from biblical history.

But the name Orpah was not to be for this tiny baby born to Vernita Lee. Either the midwife who assisted at the birth at home or the record clerk mixed up the second and third letters of the name, because *Orpah* became *Oprah* by the hand of fate—or whatever.

Oprah has said: "The midwife got the letters transposed, and I wound up Oprah on my birth certificate."

And so she became Oprah Gail Winfrey on the records—and for the rest of her life.

By the time of Oprah's birth, Vernon Winfrey was long gone from Kosciusko. It was in Alabama that he received a printed birth announcement in the mail from Vernita. There was a scrawled note for him in her handwriting:

"Send clothes!"

And that was the laid-back way he received the news of his daughter's birth.

Oprah's childhood from birth to the age of seventeen was chaotic, to say the least. It was spent in three separate geographic regions of the United States, under three disparate parental systems. These periods could be called Life with Grandmother, Life with Mother, and Life with Father.

To make it even more chaotic, those three divisions were not neatly compartmented, but tended to overlap and blur into one another. Oprah never knew from one year to the next where she might be required to live or with whom. It was not the kind of environment that might contribute to a well-integrated, stable, and easygoing personality. It took courage and fortitude even to *survive* from one move to the next.

Life with Grandmother began shortly after Oprah was born, when her mother left Kosciusko to go to Milwaukee. She had heard she could find work as a part-time maid there. The pay of $50 a week was much too high to pass up by staying in Kosciusko.

But there was no place there for a small baby. So it fell to Vernon Winfrey's mother, the sole inhabitant of a small pig farm on the outskirts of town, to take in Oprah. And she did just that.

Oprah once said: "It was my grandmother who was responsible for developing my natural talents early."

It was not a particularly easy life for Oprah, for Vernon's mother was a strict member of the Faith-United Mississippi Baptist Church and put up with very little in the way of resistance to her orders.

When Oprah was a child, the church formed a very comfortable shelter over her. She did all the things there that she should do. She was expected to read and to know Scripture first of all. Then she was expected to act in church pageants. And in addition, she was expected to recite on special occasions—when invited.

At the age of three, in fact, she made her first public appearance—speaking at the Baptist church in Kosciusko. It was Easter time, and the theme of her talk was "Jesus Rose on Easter Day." Later on that winter she gave a Christmas talk. "I was always a very articulate child," she explained.

Probably because she shone so in church, Oprah began to be called "The Preacher" by the other kids her own age. She seemed always to be *preaching* to them. They didn't like it much. They would make fun of her, announcing her arrival with a sneered "Here comes Miss Jesus," or something equally disagreeable.

Oprah hated them all. She felt it was a horrible way to be treated—but she could do nothing about it. They would spit at her in Sunday school. They did not in any way want to associate or be associated with The Preacher. Oprah Gail Winfrey was alienated at an early age—alienated and made to feel different from the rest of her peers.

She was automatically different, anyway. The level of her intelligence was far higher than most of theirs. Her natural superiority was the real reason they pushed her away and pretended to ignore her.

Ironically, Oprah had no idea that at some time in the far distant future she would be doing exactly what the kids said she was doing then—preaching. Only in the future she would be preaching not in church but from that huge international podium called television. She would be asking questions of people and be talking about life and love—and about God.

She would be a preacher who had a congregation millions of times bigger than any congregation she would have had if she had stayed in Kosciusko.

But at the time that was very far into the future—and Oprah simply felt miserable to be isolated and cast off by the people who should have been her friends. After all, she *liked* people. It wasn't right that they shouldn't like her.

In the years since her childhood Oprah has drifted from the church somewhat—but even she admits that it made a very deep impression on her young life and influenced her a great deal.

A few of her neighbors understood her better than the rest; they knew what her intelligence and brightness and shrewdness really meant—and they began saying that "the child is gifted." They would also say, "That child is *going* somewhere."

"What's so amazing," Oprah later recalled, "is that it all *happened*. I don't know why, but somewhere in my spirit I *believed* that I was going to be exactly what I am."

At that time there was only one person around—Oprah's grandmother. Vernon Winfrey's mother owned the farm and did everything there was to do to run it. She even made all Oprah's clothes herself, working laboriously with a needle, thread, and scissors.

"I never had a store-bought dress," Oprah said. "We grew everything we ate. We sold eggs." And it was very lonely out there in the country.

The house in which she lived was an ancient and dilapidated structure. "Isn't it amazing?" Oprah said recently, looking at a photograph of the house. "I remember thinking what a high porch it was, and it's only from there to there. I remember, every time I jumped off, I thought I had accomplished such a great feat. 'Whoooo, I jumped off the porch!' "

She slept with her grandmother in a huge feather bed that she will always remember. "There was an outhouse in the back. There was a well, down about a hundred yards from the house."

Oprah's primary chore was to go down there every

morning and draw water for the day. Summer, winter, autumn, and spring.

She called her grandmother "Mama," because it was the natural thing to do and also because she did not want to think about the fact that her real mother had gone to Milwaukee and left her behind. This was a bitter truth that occasionally surfaced in her mind. Resolutely, she would put it down once again.

While it was first and foremost a pig farm, the place did boast one cow and a few chickens. Aside from the pigs and those other "friends," though, Oprah was totally alone.

"The nearest neighbor was a blind man up the road. There weren't other kids. . . . No playmates, no toys except for one corncob doll. I played with the animals and made speeches to the cows."

She elaborated on that colorful bit of lore to a magazine writer. "I used to take the cows to the pasture in the morning and feed the hogs." And, of course, she got the well water each morning. "I used to do all that. But I'm thankful because I feel like I have an edge on a whole lot of other 'talk show people.' I have experienced so many different *kinds* of things."

Whatever her early life was—cataclysmic, ego-shattering, or simply bearable—Oprah survived, and sometimes, not always, she recalls it today as nostalgic and wonderful, in a kind of strange, romantic way. There she was, in that quiet rural countryside, with the total serenity of the good earth all around her. She would sit in her grandmother's lap on the front porch, watching a thunderstorm and being frightened—with her grandmother holding her tightly and explaining that "God don't mess with His children." And somehow that made it all right.

When company did come to the farmhouse—and that was seldom—Oprah's grandmother would take over. "I would be ordered to sit in the corner and keep my mouth shut." Oprah would have *loved* to talk with everybody she could—but it was just not allowed. "By the time I was three I was already talking and reading a lot." Not much else to do. "I never saw a movie, and maybe twice a year I got to see somebody's television." And that was *it*.

Grandmother was a tough taskmistress in the area of reading, writing, and arithmetic—as well as in the area of church study. In self-defense almost, Oprah soon picked up the ability to read and write. Since there was no one to read aloud to, she would spend her time with a book doing her lessons in front of the chickens and pigs.

Because Oprah was rambunctious, rebellious, and sometimes antagonistic, she was reared in what later became called "the classic rural style."

About her grandmother, Oprah once said, "She could whip me for days and never get tired. It would be called child abuse now."

But at that time in the 1950s, of course, it was all part of a normal bringing up, and not called anything bad—even by the sociologists.

One of Oprah's obsessive dreams was a most understandable and poignant one: She wished with all her heart she was white instead of black.

"I used to sleep with a clothespin on my nose, and two cotton balls. And I couldn't breathe. And all I would do is wake up with two clothespin prints on the side of my nose, trying to get it to turn up. I wanted Shirley Temple curls; that's what I prayed for all the time.

"The reason I wanted to be white," Oprah explained, "was that I never saw little white kids get the whippings I got. You spill something—you get a whipping. You tell a story, whatever happens, no matter how small the indiscretion—you get a whipping. Sometimes you got them *saved up*."

Oprah's grandmother whipped her with a switch—the term used for a small branch pulled off a tree. The part of the whipping that Oprah hated the most was where the whippee had to provide her own switch for the coming action. That meant going down the road and pulling off a branch so she could be beaten black-and-blue with it.

"It's what Richard Pryor described as the 'loneliest walk in your life'—to get your own switch! You go and pull a little limb off a tree and you bring it in."

And then—zap! pow!

"You couldn't just say, 'I won't do it anymore.' The other thing is, in the middle of the whipping, you hear, 'Now shut up, now shut up.' You couldn't even cry! You got whipped till you had welts on your back. Unbelievable. I used to get them every day because I was very precocious. I was always getting into trouble and I always thought I could get away with it.

"But you know, I am what I am because of my grandmother. My strength. My sense of reasoning. Everything. All of that was set by the time I was six years old. I basically am no different now from what I was when I was six."

She was quick and sharp, but not too interested in applying her quickness and her smartness to studies or to scholarship or that kind of thing just yet. She applied most of her wiles to making it easier for herself to cope with life as it was.

But nothing turned out to be easy. Oprah said that she probably looked sad a lot in those days. She could remember trying to find something to smile about.

"I did smile, though," she said. "I think I did. I was a *really* likable child and loved to kiss people and talk to them."

But, of course, she was not allowed to because of her grandmother's philosophy that forbade her from socializing with older people. Her grandmother's idea of bringing up a child was to keep the child in the corner, where it could be seen but not heard.

When she started kindergarten, it all seemed just a bit *childish* to her when she finally became aware of what the curriculum consisted of. None of the other kids did much of anything except string beads and draw funny pictures with crayons. Oprah then made one of her earliest rebellious protests. She wrote a letter to the teacher, informing her that she felt she didn't belong there in kindergarten.

Surprisingly enough, the teacher agreed. Oprah went back to the pigs and the chickens—*and* the books. But she had made her point, and had made it in a most unconventional and unexpected way. Kids of that age just weren't *supposed* to write letters of protest! Oprah was—different!

Shortly after that Oprah entered the first grade, and there she astounded everyone by the way she approached the subjects that came up. She seemed to know more than all the other kids put together.

She was so good, in fact, that the school skipped her from first to third grade. A lot of her rapid advance had to do with that early grandmother-initiated farm-learned ability to read and talk.

"I've been the best talker and the best reader ever since I can remember," Oprah has said—and proudly too.

By the time she got to school, she did finally make friends with a girl named Glenda Ray. Glenda lived in a house down the road from Oprah's farm—a big one made of brick and mortar. Her mother was a schoolteacher. Glenda was one up on Oprah; she had toys and real dolls—not just a corncob with toothpicks on it.

In spite of her brightness and her lucid brain, Oprah led a life that was traumatic and harsh. She never had any shoes when she was living with her grandmother in Kosciusko. In fact, she never owned a pair until she was all of seven years old—after she had left her grandmother's farm forever.

But she managed to look good, because her grandmother took very good care of her. And both her grandmother and her mother believed in looking good—no matter what a person's financial status happened to be.

Her youth was essentially a painful thing to go through. Oprah to this day can find it difficult and distasteful to discuss; usually she opts not to answer when questioned about it in any kind of detail. Except, of course, for some of the more humorous and "nice" things that happened.

Now, at the age of six, Oprah was getting to be quite a handful for her grandmother to grapple with, and about this time a big change came into Oprah's life. With the little girl exerting herself more and more in rebellion against the world around her, Vernon Winfrey's mother sought help from Vernita Lee.

The upshot of the call for help was that Oprah left Mississippi for the first time in her life and traveled to Milwaukee, where she was to live with her mother. Vernita was now making some money doing housework.

Although Oprah did not know it, she had seen the last of Mississippi—at least as a place where she would live.

It was a whole new ball game up North.

3
Life with Mother

And so began what for Oprah Winfrey could be called Life with Mother—a brief era, but a tempestuous and important one.

It was rough. On the one hand her mother worked hard to support her in Milwaukee. On the other hand, Oprah was beginning to shine as one of the "chosen" people of God—bright and aggressive and hard to manage.

She became known as "The Little Speaker," much as she had once been known as "The Preacher." She recited poems like "Invictus" at black social clubs and church teas—wherever her mother could get her to go.

But in the home with Mother—life was hell on earth.

"When I was seven I lived in Milwaukee with my mother," Oprah said. "She was a roomer with some lady." Oprah tended to be somewhat vague about certain people in her past. The woman was actually the godmother of the man who became Oprah's stepfather—her mother's husband.

"I felt like I was an outcast," Oprah recalled. "I don't know why my mother ever decided she wanted me [with her in Milwaukee]. She wasn't equipped to take care of me. I was just an extra burden on her."

The truth was that Vernita supported her daughter partly on welfare money and partly on income made by cleaning homes in some of the posh suburbs of the city.

Oprah remembered the abject poverty in which she was forced to live in that apartment her mother rented on the city's dismal Ninth Street. "We were so poor we couldn't afford a dog or cat, so I made pets out of two cockroaches," she once said in reminiscence.

She was more specific about those "pets" later. "There were lots of roaches available. You wanted pets, all you had to do was go in the kitchen at night and turn on the lights. You could find a whole family of them. So I would name them and put them in a jar and feed them . . . like kids catching lightning bugs. I called them things like Melinda and Sandy. You can't catch lightning bugs in the wintertime, so I'd keep roaches in a jar. Now I'm repulsed by the idea."

She and her mother were dirt poor. Even Vernita Lee now admits that the state of poverty described by Oprah was indeed true, but insists that "Oprah toots it up a little."

It was in Milwaukee, when Oprah was first living with her mother and the cockroaches, that she began stealing money out of Vernita's handbag.

"I wanted to have money like the other kids," Oprah said in recalling those dubious days of "doing without." "They were always saying, 'Let's go to the pizza parlor, Opie. Let's get shakes, Opie.' "

She always had plenty of names to contend with. She might be Oprah one day, Opie the next, or even Opal, Oopey, Ofra, Okra, Ofrey, Opera, or almost anything sounding like Oprah. She was even called Harpo—*Oprah* backward!

And Oprah was beginning to enjoy her success and the independence she was achieving by her rebellion. She continued to take it out on her mother at every opportunity.

Meanwhile, in the South, things were happening that

set a new chain of events into motion. Vernon Winfrey, Oprah's natural father, had left the armed forces in 1955 after serving his hitch—that was a year after Oprah's birth—and had settled down in Nashville.

Straight out of the service, without penny one in his pocket, he had arrived in town and set about scrounging a living out of two jobs—one of which Vernon later called "the worst job in Nashville." It was washing pots at one of the city hospitals. For that, he was paid the princely sum of seventy-five cents an hour! The second job was a bit more palatable—almost prestigious in comparison; he was a janitor at Vanderbilt University.

Vernon had always suffered a slight stutter, but spoke slowly and with careful deliberation to make it less noticeable. Because of his tendency to stutter, his was the image of a cautious man who believed in the innate dignity of the human being and in the old values of the church, to which he was always attached and from which he never strayed.

Soon he met "the woman" in his life—her name was Zelma—and they were married. Zelma's first pregnancy was a difficult one, complicated by several factors, and it resulted in a miscarriage. She was advised not to try to have children again.

In 1962, when Oprah was eight years old, she had become such a handful for her mother that Vernita leaped at the sudden and welcome opportunity to send her to her father and stepmother in Nashville.

When Vernon and Zelma met Oprah it was love at first sight. Although Oprah was somewhat subdued and not quite sure how things were going to work out in her new home, she did particularly like her two new parents right from the first.

"At the end of first grade, I went to live with my father and my stepmother," she said. "I had been skipped at school and was supposed to start third grade that September. My stepmother discovered I didn't know any math and was going to be in big trouble when school began."

As a result of that, Oprah was forced to spend her entire summer learning the multiplication tables—what she always termed her "times tables."

Zelma was, as Oprah explained, "real tough, a very strong disciplinarian, and I owe a lot to her because it was like military school there. I had to do book reports at home as well as in school and so many vocabulary words a week. That's what we did."

It was just like Life with Grandmother—only in this case Oprah couldn't really get away with even as much as she had been able to with her grandmother.

Unfortunately, it didn't really last all that long. Before things settled down, Oprah was uprooted once again, this time for a visit back to Milwaukee the following summer. When Vernita asked for Oprah, Vernon and Zelma agreed to the visit, of course—it was the right thing to do—but it was hard for them to part with the spirited little girl to whom they had become quite attached. Even for the few summer months she would be away.

"I moved back to live with my mother when I was nine. The reason was that my mother said, 'Come live with *me*, I'm going to get married and we're all going to be a real family.' " Vernita had been arranging to marry a Milwaukee man for years, but they had simply not yet worked it out. The man already had a son and daughter.

To Oprah, it was somewhat unnerving to be back in Milwaukee again—and once again in the zone of poverty that described her mother's life circle. At least with Vernon and Zelma, things had been fairly decent. Now she was poor again. She felt like a Ping-Pong ball, being bopped from one set of parents to another.

Summer was soon over, and right on cue Vernon arrived to take her back to Nashville for the opening of school. The meeting between Vernon and Vernita was stiff and formal. Vernita told him that she had changed her mind. She did not want Oprah to go back to Nashville. Her place was in Milwaukee, with her mother and her new father. What right had Vernon to Oprah? He had never bothered to marry Vernita, had he?

It was a difficult situation. Vernon and Zelma had recognized Oprah's need for discipline and hard work—and something of a home life to anchor it. He knew she was not getting it in Milwaukee. But there was nothing he could do, short of taking her back by force—and it simply was not in his nature to try that.

"That's why I stayed," Oprah explained. "I wanted a normal family." After all, now Oprah did have a little stepbrother and stepsister to play with. That was more normal than being all alone.

There were tears in Vernon's eyes when he said good-bye to his daughter. "We had brought her out of that atmosphere," he said later, "out of a house into a home, so I knew it was not good for her, being in *that* environment again. Oprah didn't really have much to say that night, besides hello."

And good-bye.

And so it was that what might have become her third life—Life with Father—did not begin in 1962. Oprah now was simply to live out a second part of Life with Mother back in Milwaukee, a continuation of her earlier stay there.

In fact, it was a no-win situation. "It never worked out," Oprah said. "I wanted a daddy when I was in Milwaukee. I wanted a family like everybody else because I was going to this school where kids had mothers and fathers. I used to make up stories about my mother and my dad. I told the biggest lies about them because I wanted to be like everybody else."

The truth was something else again. "I felt really ugly in this environment because the lighter your complexion, the prettier you were." At least that was true among blacks, and particularly among Oprah's family members. Her new sister, she said, "was lighter and she got all the attention, and I thought it was because she was the prettiest. I was the smartest, but no one praised me for being smart. I was teased because I was always sitting in a corner, reading; people made fun of me for that. And I felt really sad and left out. My books were my only friends."

At least she had them.

Now that she was a little bit older, she was starting to understand a great deal more about life. She was black in a world that was predominantly white; this was more obvious to her in Milwaukee than in Nashville. And she had little for herself; much of what came to the family went to her new brother and sister. Oprah was the one who always got the short end of the stick.

She began to *feel* her own alienation—not only from the mainstream, but from her natural father and her mother. To her, it seemed that *neither one of them* wanted her. She was some kind of dead weight hanging around their necks.

She started to act up in front of everybody, strike back at them. She ran away from home. Periodically. And played tricks on anybody she could.

"I started acting out my need for attention, my need to be loved," as she analyzed it later. "My mother didn't have the time. She worked every day as a maid. She was one of the maids on those buses. I was smart"—Oprah always knew that—"and my mother, because she didn't have the time for me, I think, tried to stifle it." The intelligence, that is, the smartness.

Oprah was nine years old when the tone was set for the serious "misbehavior" years that were to follow. It came about because of the cramped family conditions in which she lived.

There was a bedroom for her mother and her new father. And there was a bedroom for her and her brother and sister. Oprah had a bed for herself, and her sister and brother had theirs.

Her mother and father would invite relatives to stay overnight, and even to baby-sit with Oprah and the brother and sister when Vernita was working late or out somewhere.

Among the relatives was a nineteen-year-old male cousin —ten years older than Oprah. Instead of going home, the cousin frequently stayed over at the apartment.

"They put me in bed with him," Oprah explained later. (Actually, the cousin was put in bed with Oprah.) "There was only one bed and I had to sleep with him. Can you imagine? I didn't know anything about sex that summer."

One night her cousin simply took advantage of her and raped her in the bed. She was too naïve—too petrified—to know what was going on, too surprised to fend off this older cousin. She was left stunned and puzzled by what had happened.

The cousin knew exactly what to do. To keep her quiet about it, he took her out to visit the zoo, and bribed her there with an ice-cream cone.

"I didn't tell anybody about it because I thought I would be blamed for it," Oprah explained.

There was more to it than that, actually. Oprah came to a conclusion about what is now called "child abuse" and about the reason many abusees—the women—remain silent about it:

"I think a lot of the confusion and guilt comes to the [abused] child because [sexual intercourse] *does* feel good."

Shortly after her encounter with her cousin, when Oprah was at a playground with a school friend, the conversation got around to the way babies were made. Oprah caught on right away, even if she was only nine, and concluded that her actions in bed with her cousin were baby-making ones.

Now she had a good idea of what would happen to her! She got the idea that she was pregnant. The worst horror of the rape by her cousin was the fact that Oprah was fated to worry all through the fifth grade that she would have a baby—maybe right in class!

"Every time I had a stomachache, I thought I was pregnant, and asked to go to the bathroom so if I had it nobody could see."

It was simply *terror* to live from day to day.

"Was I going to have it? How would I hide it? All the people would be mad at me! How could I keep it in my room without my mother knowing?"

Now the already-planted patterns of misbehavior proliferated. After all, what did she have to lose now? She knew what men wanted; she knew why they wanted it; she knew they would be good to her if she gave it to them.

And so she lied. She stayed out later than her mother told her she could. She stole money from her mother's purse. She ran away from home to get dates with "everything with pants on."

After all, she *had* been raped. And there was something about sex—she even *liked* it!

In the next five years she allowed herself repeatedly to be abused by other men. At least one of them was a close friend of her mother's. Another was an uncle of Oprah's. All of the men who abused her were "trusted" members of the family—either direct blood relations or "close" friends.

Why did she allow these one-night affairs to continue? Oprah has discussed this problem many times in many different ways. "I blamed *myself*," she said in one frank interview. "I was always very needy, always in need of attention, and they just took advantage of that. There were people, certainly, around me who were aware of it, but they did nothing."

Much later, Oprah recalled the incident in this way:

"I was [some years older] when I did an interview with

someone who had been sexually abused. It was the first time it occurred to me that this thing that had happened to me had also happened to other people. I hadn't told anybody until then because I thought I was the only person it ever happened to and I thought it was my fault because afterward it happened repeatedly—with different people."

She admitted that she liked attention. And she didn't want to get anybody she knew into trouble. There would be no point to that. Besides, she would be getting herself in trouble too.

In fact, ambiguity about sex and abuse continues even to this day in her life. In a recent interview she told a reporter that she was a long way in time from Milwaukee and what had happened there. Now she could speak calmly about it from a comfortable, and safe, distance.

"I saw one of those men the other day when I went to see my mother," she admitted.

"What did the man have to say?" the reporter who was talking to her asked with great curiosity.

"Nothing," Oprah answered. "He didn't say anything."

Life in Milwaukee was not all abuse and degradation. By the time Oprah was thirteen, she was attending school in an affluent suburb of Milwaukee called Fox Point, some twenty-five miles from the center of Milwaukee.

It had been a teacher at Lincoln Middle School, where Oprah was enrolled at the time, who had given her the first boost she had ever had out of her incipient delinquence.

"Mr. Gene Abrams used to see me reading in the cafeteria," Oprah said. "He got me a scholarship to Nicolet High School."

Nicolet was a prestigious high school located on the North Shore. As an experiment in integration—it was then 1968 and the black-white cause was being fought on all educational fronts—a handful of the brightest of the black students in the city were bused out to Nicolet for their education.

It was an eye-opener for Oprah. In fact, it opened her eyes to things that she did not know about—and to things that changed her life forever.

"It was the first time that I was exposed to the fact that I was not like all the other kids," Oprah recalled. "In 1968 it was real hip to know a black person, so I was very popular."

There was one teenager named Rita whom Oprah remembered especially. She used to invite Oprah to go over to her house after school.

"Her parents would ask me if I knew Sammy Davis, Jr."

This struck Oprah as being the absolute living end. How would she ever have any way of coming to know Sammy Davis, Jr., who was a celebrated singer and comic on the nightclub circuit? How would Oprah have ever managed to wangle an introduction to him?

But it was like that all the time.

"The kids would all bring me back to their houses, pull out their Pearl Bailey albums, bring out their maid from the back and say, 'Oprah, do you know Mabel?' They figured all blacks knew each other. It was real strange and real tough."

Opening her eyes was not too good for Oprah's self-image. "I *realized* I was poor then," she said, underlining the fact that life in Kosciusko had been bare, but not really overpoweringly poverty-stricken. Life in Milwaukee *was*. "I get in the bus in the evening after school and go home and the white kids would go to the pizza parlor and drive their *cars* and stuff!

"And after seeing how the other half lived [that way], I started having some real problems. I guess you could call me *troubled*—to put it mildly."

She was, as she put it, very frustrated with the idea that she could not have what *they* had. She continued to act out her hostility. Her envy, coupled with her own hostility over the abuse of her body by trusted members of her family, caused Oprah to intensify her efforts to strike out at life around her and the individuals who peopled it.

Her mother, of course, was closer than anybody else to her—and she was the first to feel the effects of Oprah's suppressed rage.

One of the most irrational and imaginative cases of striking out indulged in by Oprah was what came to be called the "affair of the butterfly bifocals."

It started when Oprah's mother had Oprah's eyes tested and found that she was astigmatic. She was told she must wear prescription glasses—and they had to be bifocals. The pair that her mother purchased had butterfly rims on them.

"You know the bifocal lens that makes you look like a librarian used to look? I felt so bad about wearing these glasses that I said to my mother one day, I said, 'Mom, I think you need to talk about this because I'm really an *ugly* child.' "

Oprah's idea was for her mother to get her a more fashionable pair of glasses—something stylish and trendy—so Oprah would not look like such a freak. But her mother shook her head.

"No, I can't afford them."

That was too much for Oprah. She brooded about it and plotted out a scenario that was, if nothing else, at the very least ingenious.

She cut school the next morning, while her mother was out working, and threw her butterfly bifocals on the floor. Then she tramped on them until they were broken into a million pieces. She pulled down the curtains, knocked over the lamp, and then telephoned the police.

"We've been robbed!" she sobbed. "Robbed!"

It was all very dramatic. She lay down on the floor and waited for the police to arrive. When they came in, right on schedule, they took a look around and began to sense a scenario that had been slightly orchestrated. To them it just did not *look* right.

Meanwhile, Oprah was reviving from her feigned lapse into unconsciousness. Questioning her, the police began asking all the wrong questions—wrong from Oprah's point of view. To escape ignominy, she sank down into amnesia.

"Of course," she said later, "I had seen this on *Marcus Welby, M.D.*, about someone having amnesia. This was the story: Someone broke in, hit me on the head, and knocked off my glasses."

Plausible? Maybe. But the police did not buy it. After all, *they* watched television too.

Nevertheless, she was sent to the hospital and, somewhat fearful, was examined there. But luck was holding out for her. Oprah had been born with a lump on the side of her head. The intern examining her concluded that she did indeed have a concussion. The lump seemed to be evidence of that.

"How do we find your mother?" she was asked.

Oh, oh. No answer from Oprah.

"Who are you?" the doctor asked.

Oprah took that as a good reason to lose her memory once again. She went into a faint.

"Every time they'd ask me, I'd pass out again," she recalled. "I told them I didn't know!"

And all that trouble to get a new pair of glasses!

But there was more trouble to come. It came in the shape of Oprah's mother. The police of course had no trouble in locating Vernita Lee. They told her that her daughter was injured.

"I'm lying there in the hospital room," Oprah recalled. "They bring my mother in."

The almost hysterical Vernita Lee arrived with the police. She was weeping uncontrollably. They then explained to her that there had been a robbery at the apartment, and that the toughs—whoever they were—had roughed up her daughter and left her on the floor. Oh, and the robbers had broken her eyeglasses.

The tears in Vernita Lee's eyes abruptly dried up. "They broke her *eyeglasses*?" she asked in a suddenly harsh voice.

The police nodded. And they explained that Oprah apparently had lost her memory as well as her glasses.

"Uh-huh," said Vernita.

"Then the police asked me," Oprah went on, "if I knew who this was. And it was my mother."

Oprah shook her head feebly.

"You don't know who I am?" Oprah's mother asked her, glaring at her.

"No." Oprah could barely speak.

"I'm going to count to three and see if your memory improves," her mother told her slowly.

No sign from Oprah.

"One."

Nothing.

"Two."

Oprah opened her eyes. "It's coming back to me now."

Vernita glowered at her daughter, flexing her muscles.

"You're my *mother*! You're my *mother*!" Oprah hollered.

Anyway, she got the new glasses—along with a lot of sore spots on her body.

"Oprah always had big dreams," her mother recalled recently. "She was always telling me she'd go to Europe and be famous. She felt it in her bones."

Maybe she was headed in that general direction the next time she decided to run away. It was shortly after the affair of the butterfly bifocals. There was a grandiose scheme to take off forever—to kiss the old dump good-bye.

"I was going to go stay with my girlfriend," Oprah said. "I put all my things in a shopping bag, and went to my girlfriend's house."

Then they would both run away together. Or, if her

friend decided to stay home, Oprah would go off on her own.

Oprah knocked on the door.

There was nobody home at all. She had stupidly not bothered to check with her friend beforehand. The family was simply out of town on a trip—her friend with them.

"There was *nobody* there. Now what was I going to do?" Oprah wondered. Nevertheless, she was a very determined young teenager. She walked downtown into Milwaukee.

It was there that she quite fortuitously happened to be passing by when a limousine pulled up in front of a hotel and a celebrity Oprah recognized stepped out of the car to enter the lobby.

It was Aretha Franklin.

Brash and pushy, Oprah strolled up to the singer and introduced herself. Trying to hold back the tears in her eyes, she began telling the singer a hugely melodramatic story about how she had just been abandoned by her parents and needed $100 to get home to Ohio. It must have been a brilliant performance—almost as good perhaps as that which won her an Oscar nomination in *The Color Purple* some years later.

Aretha Franklin listened to the story with a straight face, and when Oprah paused for a breath between sobs, pulled out $100, no questions asked, and handed it over to Oprah. With the money in her bag, Oprah rushed over to one of the biggest hotels in Milwaukee, where she got a room and holed up in it all alone. Then she telephoned down and ordered room-service food for three whole days—until the money ran out.

"I was so scared afterward!" Oprah recalled. "I went over to my minister and confessed to him." She told him, "I am up the creek. You got to help me get back to the house!"

It took some doing, but the minister pulled it off. Oprah's mother was not particularly elated over the incident, and warned her daughter that there had better not be any more shenanigans like that, or else. . . .

The Aretha Franklin incident was far from the end, however. She continued with her imaginative forays into deep dramatics. Her little puppy, who was not properly housebroken, was ruining the carpets and floors of the apartment when Vernita finally announced to Oprah that the puppy had to go. Oprah did not see it that way at all. The puppy would stay.

Remembering the success of her earlier staged break-in, Oprah went the same route once again. The scenario was for the puppy to snap at the burglars, scare them off, and save the family jewels. In this case, Oprah began the drama by throwing all her mother's best jewelry out the window.

At that point Vernita stumbled onto the plot and quashed it. Vernita Lee had, by now, definitely *had* it with Oprah. She decided that it was all up for her. Now she had the ammunition to put Oprah in a detention home for troubled girls.

Unfortunately for Vernita and fortunately for Oprah, the home was filled at the time—there were so many other troubled youngsters—and so Oprah remained free by default.

In fact, she was so free she ran away from home again, leading her mother on a merry chase for several days, until she was located and returned to the apartment.

At that point, Vernita Lee knew that she would have to get in touch with Vernon Winfrey. She could *not* cope.

"Oprah's mother called me from Milwaukee after that and said she couldn't control her anymore," Vernon reported. Vernita explained about the detention center and the fact that it was full.

After a long conversation, it was decided that Oprah would go back to live in Nashville with her father and stepmother.

This move was to be *the* big change in Oprah's teenage life—and in her entire life-style forevermore.

"I'm grateful to my mother for sending me away," Oprah later admitted. "If she hadn't, I would have taken an absolutely different path in life."

So began Life with Father—this time for real.

4
Life with Father

The Oprah Winfrey who came down from Milwaukee to Nashville in 1968 was almost nothing like the nine-year-old girl Vernon Winfrey had reluctantly surrendered to Vernita in 1963. She had completely "grown up"—in most senses of the word. She was worldly, street-smart, unselfconscious, and dressed to the nines.

Parenthetically, Oprah Winfrey has always detested the word *street-smart* as applied to her or other blacks. "That's what they say about you when you're black to avoid saying you're intelligent," she points out. True. But in this context of her story, she was absolutely and completely "street-smart" in the generally accepted sense of the word.

Vernon and Zelma saw the heavy makeup, the short, tight skirts, and the knowing look in her eye. They saw and they shuddered. Where was the marvelous, bright little girl who had recited beautiful verses at church functions and who was such a delight to be with?

The meeting in 1968 between Vernon and Oprah was not the most inspiring or optimistic one imaginable. Instantly Vernon had his own idea about how Oprah was going to behave now that she was again under his control.

And, of course, Oprah now had her own ideas—and her own pattern of misbehavior to pursue.

The battle lines had been drawn.

It was in the stars that Vernon Winfrey was going to win that war, even if some skirmishes might go by default to Oprah. Vernon had opened a barber shop in 1964 and was now thinking of running a grocery store next door to it. He had become a successful businessman and a successful family man.

As for Oprah: "My dad really held me in with a tight rein. Without his direction, I'd have wound up pregnant and another statistic. I was definitely headed for a career as a juvenile delinquent." That was Oprah's opinion of herself at that point in her life.

Vernon has disagreed with this estimate. "She just wouldn't listen to her mother," he said. "She needed some *discipline* to make sure she got a good start in life."

And that was what Vernon vowed to give her.

What was more, he knew she was good at schoolwork, even if she did not always apply herself to it. Somehow, she needed prodding.

"Oprah was a strong child," he said, meaning that she had a good brain and knew how to use it. "You could move her out of schools in the middle of the year, and she was always able to keep up with her classmates. Oprah always could adjust to her environment."

The war started immediately—in small skirmishes and scouting encounters on both sides.

When Oprah wore a dress that had no middle and exposed her naked midriff, Vernon ordered her to remove it and put on something else.

When she put on too much makeup, Vernon sat down with her and helped her rub it off.

And whenever he caught her doing anything he did not approve of—even in the area of her language—he corrected her mercilessly.

It was his intention to become and continue to be a strict and constant presence in Oprah's life—just as strict and constant as the church to which they both belonged.

To put it in focus a bit, Vernon once explained:

"I was not the father that had to have the mother tell me, 'Well, you know, she's a girl, it's time for you to tell her things.' I talked to her about the approach of boys or men."

Winfrey said to Oprah, "If you don't hold up for yourself, the guys are not going to hold up for you."

Oprah knew the truth of that remark, even if she never let on to her father the grim details of what had happened to her in Milwaukee.

"I never knew, at the time Oprah came to live with me, that [sexual abuse] had ever happened to her," Winfrey said later. "If we had known, we might have handled her a little bit differently . . . knowing what kind of stress she was going through. But you can't always see beyond the mountain. I didn't know about that until she admitted it on her television show."

Vernon Winfrey had long talks with his rebellious fourteen-year-old daughter. He asked Oprah once, "What kind of person do you want to be?"

And before she could answer, he talked about the three different kinds of people there were: those who made things happen; those who watched things happen; and those who did not know what was happening.

"Oprah didn't like those last two kinds of people," he recalled.

In no way was Vernon the same kind of parent that Vernita Lee was. Vernon had a very clear idea of what he was doing. For the rebellious child who had been having a field day in breaking to bits all the rules and regulations her mother had set up for her, her father's way of life was a revelation.

"I knew exactly what I could and what I couldn't get

away with," Oprah said. "I *respected* his authority."

She did not realize it then, but the moment she returned to her father and stepmother was the most important one in her life, a major turning point.

"Not getting the attention from my mother made me seek it in other places—the wrong places," Oprah has said, "until my father came and got me from my mother in Milwaukee and took me to Nashville where he lived. His discipline channeled my need for love and attention into a new direction."

Moreover, she has admitted emphatically, "When my father took me, it changed the course of my life. He saved me. He simply knew what he wanted and expected. He would take nothing less."

For example, she had a habit of calling him "Pops." And Vernon objected.

"Oprah always called me 'Daddy' before she left, but when she came back to Nashville I was 'Pops.' " Vernon told her, "Oprah, honey, you were 'Gail' or 'Oprah' when you left, right? And I was 'Daddy' when you left and I'm going to be 'Daddy' since you're back. I will not accept the word 'Pops.' "

She got the message. It was "Daddy" from that day on. He had another saying that meant something to her. It was a kind of "favorite" of his:

"Listen, girl—if I tell you a mosquito can pull a wagon, don't ask me no questions. Just hitch him up!"

It was his method of demanding quick obedience.

He had a way with him that got to her. He could whip her if he chose—the way his mother, her grandmother, had always done—but he usually chose not to. Instead, she recalled, all he did was stand there and look at her hard out of the corner of his eyes with his chin down low.

He knew exactly how to exert his influence on her as strongly as possible. "I don't think she'd want to do anything too contrary to my way of thinking."

As strict as he was about what she wore and how she talked, Vernon was stricter about her education. He viewed education and learning as the key to all success.

"I remember coming home one time with *C*'s on my report card," Oprah said. "My father sat down with me."

He told her immediately, "This is not acceptable."

Oprah was indignant. "What do you mean, 'unacceptable'? A *C* is average. This is *not* a bad grade."

Vernon answered simply enough. "If you were a child who could only get *C*'s, then that is really all I would expect of you. I wouldn't demand any more from you than *C*'s. But you are not. And so in this house, for you, *C*'s are not acceptable."

That was enough for Oprah. She was smart and she was sensitive, and, above all, she had pride in her intelligence. And so she did the one thing she could do. She changed her ways.

"When my father said, 'If you don't bring *A*'s into this house from school you can't live here,' he meant it."

Zelma pitched in too, as she had before when Oprah was much smaller. She now took her teenage daughter to the library every two weeks. Whereas before Oprah had been required to read one book a week, she was now required to choose five books, read them, and write book reports about them every two weeks. *Five* in two weeks!

"Not only did I have homework from school, but homework at home!" Oprah recalled. "Plus, I was allowed an hour a day to watch television, and that hour was always before *Leave It to Beaver* came on! I hated that!" Oprah said. "But, you know, it is the absolute reason I got my first job in radio. I was hired on nothing else other than that I sounded good." And her "good" sound obviously came from her attention to the television newscasters on at that one hour of the evening that she could watch.

From all this work on her studies, Oprah developed into an *A* student. Even then, Vernon continued to fret. Now he started in on her about the fact that she never spent enough time—in *his* view—on her homework.

Actually, once she had applied herself to the principles of study, she progressed rapidly. She was simply too bright to find it necessary to spend a lot of time on it. Even so, it bothered her father that she spent so little time at her books. But when she kept coming home with those straight *A*'s, he could only shrug his shoulders.

"Daddy, what are you complaining about?" she would ask him with a twinkle in her eye.

All in all, Vernon Winfrey's way of bringing up his slightly bent and somewhat wayward teenage child was pretty straightforward and unequivocal. He later was to hang a sign in his barber shop that more or less presented his view of teenagers and their ideas of life—and, in particular, what *he* thought of those ideas. Here it is:

> ATTENTION TEENAGERS. IF YOU ARE TIRED OF BEING HASSLED BY UNREASONABLE PARENTS, NOW IS THE TIME FOR ACTION! LEAVE HOME AND PAY YOUR OWN WAY WHILE YOU STILL KNOW EVERYTHING.

On her return from Milwaukee, Oprah was enrolled in Nashville's East High School. The year was 1968. Actually, her presence at the school was all part of the city's effort to integrate the school system. She did well. People liked her; she liked other people.

She had been bright when she was young, but by now all that brightness was channeled into getting her way in almost any endeavor she attempted. Except for the strictures of Vernon and Zelma, of course.

But she continued to get *A*'s in all her subjects, just the way she had promised Vernon she would. She even won an award for oratory—another strong suit of hers. Reading and talking—those were her fortes.

When she was sixteen, without the slightest fanfare, she

was voted the most popular girl in her class at school.

What her father told her then stuck in her mind.

"Dad said, '*Anyone* can be the most popular. What about most likely to succeed?' "

(In fact, someone named "Jackie" was voted most likely to succeed in Oprah's class that year. Today Oprah frequently asks her father: "Where is Jackie today?" No answer.)

She also was urged to run for president of the high school student council. This was of course a problem for her. She was a minority among members of the majority. Her solution to that problem pointed to her future success in the world later on.

She knew that the issue of integration was high in everyone's mind in 1970, and she felt she would be ganged up on by the whites if she made a point of her race. She chose *not* to call attention to the fact at all.

When she announced her candidacy, her way to defuse the issue of race was to make it a nonissue in the campaign. She organized "cafeteria caucuses," urging voters to pick the best candidate. She even pledged better cafeteria food and improved school spirit, and touted a live band for the junior prom that year.

She won.

The year 1970 in retrospect was quite a winning year for Oprah. Not only was she tops in politics, with her new position as president of the student council, but she was selected to attend the White House Conference on Youth in Washington with a group of other students from Nashville.

She was chosen to attend because of her good grades and because she was a strong participant in high school activities and political life. In fact, in that same year, 1970, she joined the high school drama club to hone her speaking voice and polish her stage presence.

And one more important thing happened to her that

year. "When she was sixteen," Vernon said, "she went to Los Angeles to speak at a church."

This was a big event for Oprah, a trip to Hollywood. She saw Hollywood Boulevard and went to Grauman's Chinese Theatre, where the names of the stars were embedded in concrete in the front.

"She told me that she got down and rubbed the stars on the Hollywood Walk of Fame," Vernon said.

Then Oprah vowed to him: "One day, I'm going to put my star beside those other stars!"

Vernon did not laugh at her. "We knew she had great potential. We knew she had a gift and talent to act and speak when she was nine years old. She's never been a backseat person, in school or in church. She always loved the limelight."

One time when Vernon thought she was being a little too loud even for Oprah, he spoke to her about it:

"Honey, people see you when you're quiet, and they see you when you're loud. Nine times out of ten, you're better thought of when you're quiet."

After that, he said, she toned down a little bit.

But not enough to injure that natural spontaneity.

By now she had a future in mind. Seeing Hollywood had opened her eyes. Now she knew she would someday be an actress. She had all the talents that would help make her a superior stage personality: intelligence, a quick wit, a good memory, a sense of humor, an outgoing nature, and above all, imagination.

It was a terribly competitive craft, of course. She always knew that. But she was willing to fight her way up the ladder on talent alone.

Besides, even though she was black, she was amiable, bouncy, and at that time had a perfectly marvelous figure.

And sure enough it was in the very next year, 1971, that her big breakthrough came. However, it had to do with her superior abilities in the art of writing and of articulate speech—and *not* in her interest in drama. She tried out for a beauty contest to select Miss Fire Prevention for Nashville, Tennessee.

Miss Fire Prevention? Did she look good in a red hat and a fire suit?

"I know it's not a biggie," she admitted about the contest later. "But for me, it was special. I was the only black—the first black—to win the darned thing."

She won it because she had learned how to score high in the goofy question-and-answer sessions that always accompanied "beauty" contests of that kind. Those assets were always her magic key to success.

"I had marvelous poise and talent and could handle any questions, and I would always win in the talent part, which was usually a dramatic reading. I could—I still can—hold my own easily. Ask me anything, and my policy has always been to be honest, to tell the truth. Don't try to think of something to say. Just say whatever is the truth."

And so Oprah went in with nothing more than high hopes and her talent, determined to make herself look good no matter what.

On the morning of the interview with the judges, Oprah happened to tune in to the *Today* show on NBC-TV, then starring Barbara Walters.

When the judges asked her that afternoon what she wanted to do with her life, Oprah was just about to give her own well-thought-out answer—"I want to be a fourth-grade schoolteacher"—when she remembered the excitement of seeing Barbara Walters interviewing people.

"I believe in truth," she told the judges, "and I want to perpetuate truth. So I want to be a journalist."

It kept her in the contest!

There were *always* questions in these contests. Questions and more questions. In the last round of this one, the key question involved what each contestant would do if she were suddenly to come into possession of a million dollars.

By the time the judges were asking the question, the candidates had been winnowed down to three—Oprah and two others.

One contender answered the question by saying that if she had a million dollars, she would buy her mother a refrigerator, her father a truck, and her brother a motorcycle.

The second contender said that if she had a million dollars, she would give it all away to the poor.

When it came to Oprah's turn, she realized that she would be unable to top either of the other two contestants in paying tribute to altruism. They had put their money where it would help others they loved and not help themselves. That was all by the rules of the game.

She would have to attack the problem in another way. She had said she believed in truth when she had explained why she wanted to be a journalist.

"If I had a million dollars—"

They waited. The answer would determine the winner. How could she top her two competitors?

"—I'd be a spending *fool*!"

It was the sheer audacity and the humor of it that struck the judges. And it was the rightness of it, given the time and the circumstances—and the contestant. It was the first "Oprah-ism" in what was to become a long list of unforgettable one-liners in the future.

By simply stating the truth in an interesting and amusing way, she won the beauty contest!

Oprah had been sponsored for the contest by radio station WVOL, a local black outlet. As a result of winning the role of Miss Fire Prevention, she was invited to drop by the station the next day to pick up her prizes. One was a Longines watch, and the other a digital clock. Incidentally, to this day, Oprah Winfrey still has them.

"I was waiting in the lobby when a producer walked by." He recognized her and stopped to chat. One thing led to another, and finally he got interested in her.

"Would you like to hear your voice on tape?" he asked her.

"Would I?"

You bet she would.

The radio producer took her into the studio and handed her some wire copy to read.

Oprah snuggled up to the microphone and started reading from the yellow sheets. The tape rolled and her voice was on record. When she glanced up, the producer waved her on. By that time she noticed that there were two other people standing with the producer.

She continued.

By the time she was through, there were six people, including the producer, standing there listening to her carefully.

She handed back the wire copy and said, "Thanks."

They rolled the tape and listened along with her.

"You're a real good reader," said the producer.

"And the mike loves your voice," said the engineer standing nearby.

There was a brief consultation among the six bystanders. At the end of it, Oprah was asked if she would like to come down for a tryout. Maybe the station would be interested in hiring her on a part-time basis to read the news.

She was agreeable—*and* excited.

When she tried out, she was given some harder stuff to do, but of course she had no fears at all about reading. And she won the job. Actually, the job was created for her. But she was working now! Hired on the spot. It was the beginning of Oprah Winfrey on the air.

And what a beginning!

She was a big shot at school—and she was in radio!

Every afternoon she would rush away from high school, do the news at 3:30, 4:00, and every half hour until 8:00 at night. It was a marvelous life!

Reading was, as always, a breeze for her.

Between news stints on the air, she would spend a lot of time on the telephone with friends. She was once chatting animatedly to her current boyfriend about very personal things when the station manager dropped in to point out that she had left the mike open and was spreading her personality all over the Nashville area.

Later on Oprah Winfrey was to discover that broadcasting the news on radio wasn't really *her* thing. But it was some time before she found that out—and in between, a lot happened to her. Some of it was good, some of it was not so good, and some of it was downright bad.

High school graduation was approaching, and by now Oprah knew what she wanted out of life. She wanted to kick loose from Nashville, get away from the South. She would like to go to some remote college campus to see what life was really like there, rather than what it was like in Tennessee.

It was Vernon Winfrey who put the damper on that idea. Certainly Oprah was college material; no one knew that better than he. But he did not want her to go away from home. He said that there was plenty for her to learn right here at home, in Nashville. If she went off somewhere else, there was no telling how she would fare.

Vernon Winfrey knew his daughter. He knew that the most important thing for her was to be kept on a tight rein. If she was too far away, he would be unable to exert any pressure on her. She needed most of all a firm hand.

He would guide her through the difficult years of late adolescence. He had sworn to do so after getting her back from her mother in Milwaukee. That might make up for her lapses in her early teen and preteen years.

Oprah was smart enough to realize that her father was right. But she felt insulted that he wanted to continue to keep close watch on her. She was annoyed that he was still clinging to her, still bossing her around. In the end, though, she surrendered to his dictates. She would go to college somewhere nearby—probably somewhere in Nashville. There were a lot of good colleges in the area.

In her senior year there was another contest. This one was sponsored by the local Elks Club. Vernon talked his daughter into trying out for it. It was a beauty contest, but this one had a prize that was impressive. Whoever won would get a four-year scholarship to Tennessee State University, right there in Nashville.

Needless to say, Oprah Winfrey won the contest, hands down.

5
College Days

College for Oprah Winfrey turned out, unfortunately, not to be precisely what the doctor ordered. In fact, unlike high school, where she blossomed, college proved to be a distressing and nonproductive period in her personal life.

Nevertheless, her momentum from high school—student-council president, most popular senior, prize-winning orator, part-time news anchor on a local radio station, and recipient of a full scholarship to college—continued during her freshman year.

She was hardly just another first-year co-ed. It was in that first year that her expertise in beauty contests gained her another big win. This one pitted her against other black women for the title of Miss Black Tennessee.

"I didn't expect to win," she said, "nor did anybody else expect me to. There were all these light-skinned girls—vanillas—and here I was a fudge child—real dark-skinned. And Lord, were they upset, and I was upset for them. Really, I was."

"Beats me, girls!" she told them when it was all over and the ruffled egos had all been stroked. "I'm as shocked as you are. I don't know how I won either."

No?

She won because she licked the competition where she was strongest—in *personality*. The poise, the confidence, the cool manner.

She admitted later: "I won on poise and talent. I was raised to believe that the lighter your skin, the better you were. I wasn't light-skinned, so I decided to be the best *and* the smartest." To make up for her "inferior" shade of darkness, of course.

She won the contest, but, from that high, Oprah's college career was, unfortunately, a downer.

She even tried out for another beauty contest—the one held to choose Miss Black America. But this time she did *not* win.

"I didn't do well at all," she explained. "The girl from California who *stripped* won."

Things were beginning to go bad all over for her. She was much sought after by the young men of Nashville. After all, she was a good-looking, nubile woman with a smashing figure. At the time she won the Miss Tennessee beauty contest, she weighed only 135 pounds.

"You could see my *bones,*" she said later.

The temptations thrust in her way were many. Oprah would dramatize the situation in the years to come by telling groups of teenage youngsters about her battles with sex.

"I have been in the backseat with some Negro with his hand on my breast, talking about, 'Baby, you don't have to,' in one breath, and the next minute saying, 'If you love me, you really *would.*' But, had I not said no, I could be in a position that would never have allowed me to be able to do the things and be all that I can be right now."

It was difficult to pass up those ordinary pleasures; after all, falling into that "normal" routine was acceptable. But she was conscious of her worth—and somehow managed to salvage it for better things.

It was that same year—1971—that she almost dropped out of the race for success. She fell in love with a young man named William Taylor. Now a mortician in Nashville, he was the most interesting person in her young life. With her college career only beginning, and her relations with her college peers not yet established—and with her good looks a burden rather than an asset in this situation—she almost fell into the marriage trap.

"I'd be married to a mortician and probably be teaching Sunday school in Nashville someplace," she would tell her teenage audiences later. "Lord, I wanted him! Oh, I wanted him!"

She wanted him, but he was an inveterate singles player. He did not really want her *enough*.

A crisis came in their relationship, and he threatened to walk out on her. To try to keep him there with her, she even threw his keys down the toilet. She then threatened to jump out of a window into the street if he did not stay with her.

"I wanted him! I was on my knees *begging* him!" she confessed later, with some shame.

The scene was an emotional one, and Oprah was devastated when Taylor finally walked out on her, telling her that marriage to her simply was *not* in the cards.

And Oprah?

For days she wept bitterly.

He left her—and in the future Oprah would roll her eyes and say: "To this day, I thank *God* he left!"

Recovering from this emotional trauma was not easy for Oprah. Her schoolwork suffered. She was unhappy with the way her life was going. And at the same time, she found that her college career was turning completely sour.

For her, this was indeed a strange turn of events. Normally a bright person—like Oprah Winfrey—will enter college and find his or her horizons expanded beyond imagination, and will come out of the four-year stint with renewed interest and recharged energies.

Not so Oprah.

Why not?

For the moment it is important to see exactly what was happening in the rest of the country rather than dwell merely on the close confines of Oprah's personal life.

The decade of the 1960s had just ended, but the hopes raised in the black community by that stormy period of progress had not really come yet to full fruition. A sense of frustration was beginning to set in—a sense of outrage that the full equality promised by those revolutionary years was not being fully, or even partially, realized.

To recap:

The first move to achieve racial integration, the declaration by the Supreme Court that racial segregation in public school was unconstitutional, had occurred in 1954 during the Eisenhower administration.

In 1955 the second move occurred when Rosa Parks refused to give up her seat to a white man on a bus in Montgomery, Alabama. This act of defiance, followed by a boycott and protests by black groups, led to the declaration of bus segregation as unconstitutional by a federal court.

To protect black voting rights, Congress moved in 1957 to pass the first civil rights bill for blacks since the Reconstruction years of the nineteenth century. In that same year, nine black students entered Central High School in Little Rock, Arkansas, after being blocked by Governor Orval Faubus. President Eisenhower sent federal troops to enforce integration. That was a first.

In 1960 four black college students in Greensboro, North Carolina, refused to move from a Woolworth's lunch counter when denied service. More than seventy thousand students, white and black, participated in protest sit-ins in various parts of the country.

In 1962 James Meredith enrolled as the first black student at the University of Mississippi, but only after three thousand troops were called in to put down riots caused by Meredith's appearance on campus.

In 1963 the civil rights movement peaked when two hundred thousand people marched on Washington, seeking equal rights for blacks. At the climax of the demonstration, Dr. Martin Luther King, Jr., gave his famous speech:

> I have a dream that . . . this nation will rise up and live out the true meaning of its creed—"we hold these truths to be self-evident, that all men are created equal."

In 1964 three civil rights workers were murdered in Mississippi; seven men were eventually convicted of conspiracy in their deaths. That same year, a so-called omnibus civil rights bill was passed by Congress that banned discrimination in voting, in jobs, in public accommodations, and in other areas.

In 1965 Watts, a suburb of Los Angeles, erupted into a racial riot in which thirty-five persons were killed and $200 million worth of property was torched.

In 1967 twenty-six people were killed in black riots in Newark, New Jersey, and fifteen hundred injured. In Detroit, forty were killed, and two thousand injured, with five thousand left homeless by looting and burning.

In 1968 Martin Luther King, Jr., was assassinated in Memphis; Senator Robert F. Kennedy was shot in Los

Angeles after celebrating his presidential-primary victory there.

This was the peak of the sound and the fury of the movement. All these crucial events, it will be noted, had occurred during the lifetime of Oprah Winfrey. The black world was deeply and critically involved in these radical changes. It could not help but be.

While in 1971 the heat of the excitement had died down somewhat, the movement was still alive all around her. It seemed to be everywhere. She herself had recognized its power when she had run for office in high school. And she now knew full well what it was to be black in a world of whites. After all, she had spent some years living in Milwaukee.

Of course she believed in the rights of blacks in the white world of America. Of course she was conscious of black power. Of course she stood for making way for upward mobility of all blacks.

But early on, at the age of fourteen, in 1968, she had once heard Jesse Jackson speak. And Oprah always remembered his charge.

"He said that excellence was the best deterrent to racism and sexism; that the greatest contribution you can make to women's rights, to civil rights, is to be the absolute damnedest best at what you do. That became my philosophy."

But when, after winning her four-year scholarship from the Elks Club, she entered Tennessee State University, Oprah found to her dismay that she had been deluded somewhat about what to expect from a college career.

Tennessee State University was an all-black college. It was still in the throes of the civil rights movement. Oprah was interested in dramatics and speech—both pursuits she felt could further her career in the theater, in radio, or in television.

Frankly, she could not have cared less about politics. And yet— And yet— Her attitude caused problems—big problems—from the moment she walked on campus.

"It was a weird time," she said later. "This whole black-power movement was going on then, but I just never had any of those angry black feelings. I tried to do the 'Hey, brother' bit, but it was a sham. Truth is, I've never felt prevented from doing anything because I was either black or a woman."

To sum it up:

"The other kids were all into black power. I wasn't a dashiki kind of woman."

It was therefore a trying period in her life. Although she worked hard at it, she simply was unable to get up any tremendous enthusiasm about the burning issues of the day. She wanted to study. Drama. Speech. English.

How did the other blacks react to her apolitical attitude?

"They all hated me—no, they *resented* me. I refused to conform to the militant thinking of the time."

One of the problems, she felt, was that she was in the middle of an all-black community confined to the borders of the campus. In that isolated atmosphere, there was nowhere she could go to neutralize the antagonism that surged around her.

"For four years everybody was angry," she said. "It was *in* to be angry."

Oprah did not have the temperament to waste her energy in blowing off steam against something that she felt —*knew* in her bones—could not be altered by the blowing off of steam.

"Race is not an issue with me. It has never been an issue with me. In school, when the other black kids were organizing a bloc vote for student council, I couldn't work with them because I thought their candidate wasn't the best qualified. I was ostracized then; they called me 'Oreo.' "

And she had her own ideas about race and race relations.

She, who had come up from the worst sort of environment, had been able to make her way—not, of course, without the help of her natural father and stepmother. But she *had* made her way. She had discovered that by using her head, by trying to make the best of herself, she could get ahead. She resented the fact that the others around her were really throwing away their opportunities by harping on the same old theme. To her it was the worst form of self-indulgence.

"Whenever there was any conversation on race, I was on the other side, maybe because I never felt the kind of repression other black people are exposed to. I think I was called 'nigger' once. When I was in the fifth grade."

Needless to say, this attitude did not make her popular among her classmates at college. She simply attended class, studied on her own, and spent most of her time by herself.

"I hated, *hated*, HATED college! Now I bristle when somebody comes up and says they went to Tennessee State with me."

After her breakup with William Taylor, she studied hard and worked at her courses with an industry and energy that surprised even her father. She knew he felt that she was wasting her time in speech and drama.

"I'm not sending you to school to become an actress," he told her when she first announced what her major and her minor were going to be.

After all, he knew that she had once said she wanted to be a fourth-grade teacher. What had happened to all that good ambition? he wondered.

And it was true. "I wanted to be my fourth-grade teacher for a long time," Oprah explained. "I wanted to be Mrs. Duncan. Fourth grade was the turning point in my life—I discovered long division!"

The point was, by the time Oprah was in college, she was positive about what she *really* wanted. She definitely wanted to be an actress. She was good in speech and drama—she had *always* been able to read quickly and intelligently and with the proper expression. Besides, she was quick on her feet and good at extemporaneous speaking.

She also knew that she had one of the toughest of all rows to hoe because of her color—the color black, in general, but the actual *shade* of blackness that she was.

"There are fudge brownies, gingerbreads, and vanilla creams," was the way she explained it. "I'm a fudge brownie." She meant that blackness came in as many different shades as all the other colors combined.

"The vanilla creams are the girls who could pass if they wanted to. I mean, they're sort of borderline. Gingerbreads are the girls who, even though you know they're black, have all the features of white women—the lips, the nose, maybe even a green eye here and there.

"The fudges? No doubt about it. We are black women. You will never see *me* and say, 'Gee, I wonder if she's mixed. I wonder if she's Puerto Rican.' You say, '*There*—now *there*—is a black woman.'

"In society, as little black children, we were taught that the browner you were the tougher time you were going to have in life. So a lot of little blacks are born and their parents look at them and say, 'We'll educate her.' That's what they did with me!"

In fact, Oprah once confessed that her own coloring had a lot to do with where she went to college in Nashville.

"There was another black college [not Tennessee State University] where *all* the vanilla creams went. I thought it was a better school, but I wouldn't go, just because I didn't want to have to compete with the vanilla creams because they always got the guys."

Fudge brownie or vanilla cream, Oprah was working harder at college than she had ever worked in high school, or in junior high, or even in grammar school. Because of her apolitical bent, she was more or less isolated from her peers—and because of that, she did not really take as active a part in the collegiate social world around her as she might have had she been more politically oriented, more accepted. Instead, she parlayed her apolitical bent into a very good-paying job.

There was a job opening at WTVF-TV in Nashville, the CBS television outlet there. Since she was already used to working on radio at WVOL, it seemed a natural thing that she should try out for that job.

But Oprah had almost made up her mind at that point to work steadily toward one career only: that of acting. She was not a reporter, not a journalist, nor a radio announcer or television commentator.

But it did seem the obvious way to go at the time. After all, she was experienced in reading the news on the air. Experience always helped. And the folks at WTVF-TV knew about her. They had caught her on WVOL.

"They called me three times," Oprah said. But she told them at first that she did not want to try out because she was in college and she was going to be serious about her studies. That meant she would continue with her classes and forget about television.

They called again, and again.

In some quandary, Oprah went to her speech teacher and told him what was bothering her. She wanted to continue her studies. If she got a job, she would have to quit, wouldn't she?

The man stared at her aghast. So stunned was he that he almost fell apart. "I've seen some *stupid* people," he boiled over at Oprah. "Don't you know that's *why* people go to college? So that CBS can call them?"

She got the message. And she also got the station on the phone and made an appointment for a tryout.

"I had no idea what to do," she said. "So I pretended to be Barbara Walters. It seemed *she* was my only mentor. I used to watch the *Today* show, and I thought, 'I'll do what Barbara does.'

"I would sit like Barbara, or like I imagined Barbara to

sit, and I'd look down at the script and up to the camera because I thought that's what you do, how you act. You try to have as much eye contact as you can—at least it seemed that way from what I had seen Barbara do."

Whatever she did, she did it right. She impressed the station brass and they hired her.

Vernon Winfrey was not at all put out by the idea that his daughter was working while she was in college. In fact, he was stunned to learn that she was making as much money as she was. She was salaried at $15,000 a year—while still a college student!

As for the problem of attending classes *and* holding down her important job at the station—it simply never materialized. There was always ample time for her to do her college work *and* to handle the news after class hours.

Still, it was not at all easy to work into this tough television job. She knew she was a fudge brownie, one who photographed blacker than lighter blacks. She knew she was quick, and sharp, and smart—but maybe she was just a bit *too* sassy to do the job well.

What she did, of course, was to fall back on the Barbara Walters formula for her own new image. She *became* Barbara Walters II, looking into the camera the same way she did, making little nods—and she survived.

Even so, she later confessed that it took her a very long time to get some sense of herself on camera. She would study tapes of herself reading the news, and try it different ways to get that self-conscious look off her face.

Always, of course, she knew that she had gotten the job because of the big push in the country to hire minorities. "Sure I was a token," she admitted later. "But I was one *happy* token."

Happy she may have been, but not particularly over her ability to do the news.

"I really agonized," she said later. "I was a horrible writer." She tried to improve her style, but she seemed too stiff to write down the words that *sounded* good. She was always better at the ad lib than at the preconceived think piece. "But I stuck it out."

She was indeed subliminally developing the distinctive Oprah Winfrey image at the time, but she did not know it then.

"The problem was that you can't pretend to be somebody else for *too* long," she pointed out. "You need to develop your own sense of style. So sometimes I'd forget to be Barbara, and *Oprah* would start slipping through.

"I felt that being Oprah was certainly more comfortable for me, but in the beginning, being Barbara was what saved me, because otherwise I'd have been petrified."

She knew that if she acted like Barbara Walters—because Barbara was on television and she was doing all right, wasn't she?—then she, Oprah, would be all right and last too.

She was the first female *and* the first black newscaster in Nashville. Later she was promoted to anchor the six o'clock news—while she was still a senior in college!

She graduated in 1976, and became a full-time news anchor at the CBS outlet. Still, in spite of her success, there were problems in her life.

It was becoming difficult for Oprah to stay in Nashville. She knew that the answer to her future did not lie in Tennessee at all. But it was hard to get away from home.

In the long run, it was the stricture of her home life that finally gave her the impetus to leave.

In fact, she left for personal reasons—not for professional ones.

The ironic situation was that Oprah Winfrey was earning a good five-figure salary as anchorwoman on WTVF-TV, Nashville. And yet at the same time her father had her on a strict midnight curfew.

And with Vernon, "strict" was "*strict*-strict." That meant

Oprah could not miss the midnight curfew, or else. . . . To stay out later, or to go to a party, Oprah had to let Vernon know her escort's name and the names of all the guests at the party!

"He was the kind of a father who said, 'Be home by midnight, or, by God, sleep on the porch!' And he meant it."

She began looking around. She sent her tapes to Los Angeles and to Boston and to New York.

She struck pay dirt in a most unexpected place.

It was Baltimore, Maryland.

6
Baltimore Anchor

Nashville, Tennessee, was a city of 455,651, the capital of the state, and an educational center boasting Vanderbilt University and Fisk University, in addition to Tennessee State University. Nevertheless, Oprah Winfrey's move from Nashville's WTVF-TV to Baltimore's WJZ-TV was a big step in the general direction of big-time broadcasting.

Baltimore was a much bigger city than Nashville—about half again as large. Its population was 787,775. It was, in fact, the tenth-largest city in the United States. It also had a much more prestigious history than Nashville. Settled in the seventeenth century, it was the place where Francis Scott Key had composed the national anthem during the bombing of Fort McHenry, and in the 1970s was known nationally for its major urban redevelopment project in the downtown area.

Although Oprah had always wanted to make it big in a place like New York—who wouldn't?—she was happy for the chance to prove herself in Baltimore. She was confident and feisty when she arrived at WJZ-TV, the city's ABC outlet, and anxious to show the people what a good newscaster she was. She would, she felt, out-Barbara Barbara Walters!

To celebrate her independence from the strictures of Vernon Winfrey's authority, she made it a point to attend a staff party at the station almost on the day she arrived in town, and to underline her own degree of personal freedom and self-worth, she stayed up until dawn—waiting for that old magic that would transform her into her own woman. Just like Cinderella—in reverse.

There was no magic.

In fact, the way the job at WJZ-TV developed, it became obvious to Oprah that exactly the reverse of magic was about to befall her. Reading the news in Nashville somehow was not quite the same thing as reading the news and being a co-anchor in Baltimore.

There were many reasons why the special magic failed to strike in this new and challenging job.

Whatever, she waded right in, in typical Oprah fashion. From the moment she was hired, she was scheduled to act as co-anchor for the six o'clock evening newscast. She was a promotable item, and the station began immediately to mount a public-relations campaign, giving the city of Baltimore something to think and talk about. Billboards all around the city and environs soon sprouted up with the "cute" and somehow leading question

WHAT'S AN OPRAH?

It did *not* amuse Oprah. From the beginning she loathed the publicity angle of the cutsey-pie "what's-it?" phrase.

"I think it hindered me," she said, referring to the city-wide campaign. "It was *calculated* on their part. It's best if you get to know the city first, if people get to like you on your own merits, by word of mouth." To raise the question and direct attention to Oprah in that fashion seemed unproductive and wrong-way-to.

There was another reason for the lack of magic. Oprah

was paired off with a veteran newscaster named Jerry Turner on the evening show. It was, as one *Baltimore Sun* reporter, Luther Young, wrote in a story about the two co-anchors, "a marriage which quickly failed."

Well, to get back to the question—what, indeed, *was* an Oprah?

First of all, she was black, and that was a plus at the time. She had everything going for her. But somehow, none of it seemed to come together at the right time.

For one thing, as she later said, referring to the relationship on camera between her and her male co-anchor, "The chemistry left a lot to be desired." As, indeed, became apparent to others at the station and in the audience watching them.

Nor was she particularly sanguine about her own talent at that point. When it was clear that she still had a few things to learn about broadcasting in general, something came apart inside her.

"I was so naïve I thought you could just go on the air and do the best you could."

That was true, of course. But no matter how hard she tried, she simply could not get herself to come over right.

For one thing, she had never had much training in going out on a news story and digging around for details and bringing it back in a polished, finished manner. She knew she was a lousy writer. What was more crucial, she had never learned how to adapt herself to the most salient point in journalism—*distancing* oneself from the story in such a manner that one can present it as something outside oneself.

The problem was with Oprah Winfrey's persona. She *really* wanted to be an actress—a person whose job it was to *show* emotion and to *live* a story. She never really wanted to be *outside* things that were happening, an observer equipped with the cold-blooded objectivity necessary to *tell* what was really happening. She found that she was automatically projecting her own persona onto the people with whom she was talking and in that way insinuating herself into the subject of the story.

"I really wasn't cut out for the news," she said later in a frank analysis of her co-anchor failure. "I'd have to fight back the tears if a story was too sad." To put it in another way, "I just didn't have the proper reportorial detachment."

One case in point was a dramatic story to which she was assigned. She was required to interview a woman after a fire had destroyed her home. When Oprah got to the scene of the fire she found the woman, grief-stricken, wandering about almost in a daze. When Oprah telephoned back to the station that the story was too sad for her to handle, her boss blew up. If she didn't bring back the story, he told her, she would be fired. It was her *job* to get the story—no matter *how* sad it was!

Oprah set herself to the task and began to question the woman. The victim had lost everything she had ever owned in the fire, she told Oprah. And—worse was to come. She had lost seven children in the blaze—all of them were *dead*.

Oprah simply burst into tears on hearing this.

When she brought the taped story in to the station, she told her boss that it was too painful to show, but he rolled the tape and disagreed. Under direct orders, she went on the air with it, watched it as the tape played, and apologized to her viewers at the end for the way she had handled it—for being unable to do it objectively.

"It was not good," she confessed later, "for a news reporter to be out covering a fire and crying with a woman who has lost her home. I knew from the beginning that I was only a performer. To a great extent that's what telling the news is—a performance. But news people will tell you that it's not *performing* at all."

Oprah could only be herself on the air.

"So it was very hard for me to all of a sudden become

'Ms. Broadcast Journalist' and not *feel* things. How do you *not* worry about a woman who has lost all seven children and everything she's owned in a fire? How do you *not* cry about that?

"Or, you're at a plane crash and you're standing right there and you're smelling the charred bodies, and people are coming to find out if their relatives are in the crash. And they're weeping, and you weep too because it's a tragic thing."

But her bosses didn't think so.

"So I recognized that I had a problem. But I still remained a reporter. That's what I was hired to do. For a long time I continued as a reporter and an anchorwoman."

But, in her opinion, not a very good one. For one thing, she did not like to read the news copy ahead of time to check for errors or words she might mispronounce. To her there was a great deal to be said for a "spontaneous" experience—that is, "getting the news when everybody else got it."

As a result of that, names were occasionally butchered, or grammar or diction fell by the wayside. Her reputation began to suffer as it became obvious that she was simply reading the stories for the first time, more or less performing a sight-reading exercise for the amusement of the viewers.

Eventually even the station began to recognize the seriousness of Oprah's weaknesses and began to agree with her own estimate of herself—one she had felt instinctively from the beginning. They could see it for themselves now as they watched her on-air performance.

First of all there was the now-famous "case of the mispronounced word." That was the beginning of the end for Oprah as a co-anchor on the six o'clock news. The word she butchered was a very simple one—Canada. How could anyone mispronounce "Canada"?

Oprah did. She said it and it came out all sideways and

upside down. Wrong accent. Wrong diction. Awful. But Oprah did not apologize. Actually, it was and is television and radio policy never to point out an error. Simply sail right on as if nothing has happened.

Oprah violated all the rules.

She heard herself murder "Canada"—and she laughed.

Then she said it again and got it right.

It was the laugh that was taboo. And yet for Oprah it opened her eyes to what she had quite instinctively done. An automaton reading of the news had suddenly become a live thing.

"It was the first time I had shown any resemblance to truth on the air," she said. "Before that, I was a Twinkie doll. Everything was done for me—the script, how I should look, how I should talk. It was all, 'Thank you, Jerry, and now back to you, Bob.' I was *pretending* to be something. I wasn't real.

"When you're lying, your spirit is uncomfortable. I'm grateful for those years. I always knew it was a means to an end. But I couldn't be an objective anchor reading words written for me by someone else."

The station knew it too. And the brass began to fret about Oprah. She had a solid contract with the station, and it was in six figures. It had to be honored. What to do with her? It was obvious she was not *right* as a six o'clock anchor.

This episode led to a few other "breaks"—ad-libbing—on the part of Oprah. Because she knew that she was coming over better as a natural person rather than as a robot, she began to elaborate a little on the news stories that she was reading.

"I'd never read the news in advance," she recalled, "and it made the news director angry. I'd be reading something and break in to say, 'Wow, that's terrible!' All my reactions were getting to be real. It was a kick to me. It wasn't organized."

Of course, this was not the brass's idea of how the news

should be handled. It was, in effect, *editorializing* on the items. In this objective trade, that was a no-no.

Management *had* to act. And it did.

On April 1, 1977—April Fools' Day!—they called her in and Oprah got the word that she was going to be removed from the anchor spot.

It was a demotion, of course. Something bad for the ego, as well. The station was adamant. It would have to figure out something *else* for her to do. Meanwhile, she was an anchor without a slot.

Because she did not fit into the role for which she had been hired, the station finally came up with a strategy. The problem, the brass felt, was that Oprah didn't fit the slot —not that the slot was the wrong one to try to fit her into in the first place. Thus, the obvious thing to do was to change Oprah!

Brilliant.

Television is an intimate medium of communication. Communication depends on appearance and on voice. Oprah's voice was okay, but her appearance—

Well, she was black. That was good. But perhaps *she* was not really a black-is-beautiful person. In an inspired stroke, the station decided to take her in hand and make *cosmetic* improvements.

It was the assistant news director who gave it to her with both barrels one morning. He sat her down opposite his desk and stared at her a long moment before coming out with it.

"Your hair's too thick," he told her. "Your eyes are too far apart. Your nose is too wide. Your chin is too long. You have to do something about it."

There it was, all out in the open. The assistant news director leaned back in his chair with a self-satisfied look. After all, he had solved the problem. The ball was now in Oprah's court.

She was devastated. She sat there in an absolute funk. After all, she had won beauty contests. It wasn't as if she were some kind of plug-ugly. Besides that, the station had seen what they were getting when they hired her. Why didn't they hire a woman with thin hair, with narrow eyes, with a needle nose, with a receding chin? Why had they hired her? Just to humiliate her?

"What am I supposed to do about it?" she asked from the depths of her shattered ego.

"We're going to send you to New York to an exclusive and expensive beauty salon. Not everybody is as lucky as you."

And so Oprah, trying to rejuvenate her shot-down ego, traveled to Manhattan and entered the salon of a makeup artist, who fooled around with her face for a while, gave her some eyeliner and eye shadow and a lot of tips on how to make herself look not like an Oprah but like something else "fashionable."

The next step was a hair salon. After all, the dictum was that her hair was too thick. They were obviously going to thin it. Trying to remain calm, Oprah sat there while they studied her.

"I ended up in this one place," she said later. "They did chichi poo-poo makeovers. They gave me a French perm. A French perm and Negro hair don't mix. When you go into a salon and they all speak French—take my advice and *get the hell out of there, toot sweet!*"

The experts huddled around her, stared at her, felt her hair, and so on. They discussed the situation in French and English in terms that Oprah did not understand or care to understand. After several hours of important high-level consultation, they began to work on her.

The idea was to give her the French permanent wave she mentioned. Her hair was too thick for the usual chemicals, and of course the experts had to decide what to substitute for them. Eventually they came to a conclusion and Oprah went on the table.

From the beginning, the operation was uncomfortable. Oprah was not happy, she was not easy, and she was not self-possessed.

"I felt the lotion burning my skull," she said. "I kept telling them, 'Excuse me, this is beginning to burn a little.' Hell, it wasn't burning—it was *flaming!*"

This did not faze the salon *artistes*. "Oh, just a few more minutes," they told her. After all, her hair was thick; it needed powerful chemicals to straighten it out.

"I was such a mouseburger," Oprah said, "that I actually sat there afraid to say anything while my scalp was burning up!"

When she came out from under the dryer, she thought it looked awful. But the chichi operators were ecstatic. "It's beautiful!"

She went back to Baltimore.

Something dramatic began to happen. Her hair started to loosen from her skull. It was actually thinning out. Bull's-eye! The experts had been right. Yeah—it was getting thinner and thinner and thinner and thinner—

"In a week," Oprah reported, "I was bald!" As bald as the great American eagle! Oprah described herself as "billiard-ball bald."

This was a crushing blow not only to Oprah but to the television brass as well. *Thin* hair was okay, but—an eggshell-smooth skull?

The obvious thing to do was to put on a nice wig and do the show in it. Whatever show they decided to put her on.

As is the case in many such instances, the obvious simply did not pan out.

"There's not a wig *made* to fit my head," she explained. After all, she had been born with that bump on her head.

And that bump more or less altered the circumference, making her head an extra-extra-extra-jumbo large.

"It's twenty-four and a half inches around!" she said. "So I had to walk around wearing scarves for months. All my self-esteem was gone. My whole self-image. It was horrible. I cried constantly."

No show. The threat of no job. No future. But most of all—no hair! No Oprah!

"You learn a lot about yourself when you're bald," Oprah summed it up later. "I went through a real period of self-discovery. You have to find *other* reasons for appreciating yourself. It's certainly not your looks."

The only person who proved a support to her during this trying crisis-ridden time was a reporter named Lloyd Kramer, who later left for NBC-TV in New York.

"Lloyd was just the *best*. That man loved me even when I was bald! He was wonderful. He stuck with me through the whole demoralizing experience. That man was the most fun romance I ever had."

Gradually her hair came back in. At least it hadn't been totally destroyed by the French-speaking *artistes* at the Big Apple salon. But her ego took a long time recovering from that fiasco.

"They wanted to make me a Puerto Rican. Or something. What I should have said then, and what I would say now, is that nobody can tell me how to wear my hair. I've since vowed to live my own life, to always be myself."

Back at the station the program directors were still trying to devise something for Oprah to do. The money they were paying her was simply going down the drain. She *had* to work somehow to pull her weight.

Back to basics. The two things a television communicator *had* to have was image and speech. If image couldn't be fixed, then perhaps speech could be.

And now the brass decided to try to rejuvenate the image of Oprah as a communicator by giving her a short stint with a speech coach in New York—to make her a viable communicant in Baltimore broadcasting.

Touché! In principle, it sounded just great!

Oprah went into *this* misadventure with a grim determination to make a success of it. She was tired of being linked to failure. And the project started out very well. The coach found immediately that she had a bright and talented woman on her hands, not some dull beauty of a Barbie doll.

The voice coach rightly reasoned that there was something else besides verbal diction that was not quite right at the station, and that the root of the problem Oprah was facing might lie somewhere other than in her speech.

The voice-improvement lessons altered course shortly after they began, becoming something quite different. The program turned into a kind of psyching-up-of-the-persona project. The coach turned into a rooting section for Oprah, rather than a therapist for her speech patterns.

She rightly concluded that Oprah was not standing up for herself with enough determination to override the decisions being made by her employers—most of them the wrong ones.

"You'll never make it in broadcasting unless you toughen up!" she told Oprah. "You can't let them push you around like this! Stand up and fight for your rights!"

Oprah listened, but did not act.

"They're going to chew you up and spit you out because you're too *nice*!"

Oprah was puzzled over this assessment of her personality. After all, that was what she had always tried to be—nice.

"I wanted people to think I was a *decent* girl." She was a decent girl—and yet look what was happening to her!

The speech therapist finally graduated her back to the television moguls who were paying her bills, announcing that the therapy was concluded. That was all right with

Oprah. But when she came back to the station, the same old problems began to surface once again.

What could they do with Oprah Winfrey? Hell, it even said it on all the signs—

WHAT'S AN OPRAH?

That, once again, seemed to be the primary question. It was, in Oprah's later estimation, "the whole Christine Craft syndrome. They tried to change me into something I wasn't."

Of course, it did not work.

Nevertheless, one last desperate move remained. The station finally made it.

It was a makeshift move at best. Oprah was slated to co-host a short local fill-in show in the morning called *People Are Talking*.

Would she be any better at talking than at reading?

It did not seem so to anyone in the know—but they would certainly try it.

After all, *something* had to be done.

7
Oprah Is Talking

People Are Talking was a kind of low-key early-morning talk show—slotted in as a continuation of the very successful network show on ABC-TV called *Good Morning America*.

Oprah went into it without any of her usual confidence or feeling of certain success. In fact, she was almost humble when she showed up for the job. After all, she could well be seeing the end of her television career—such as it was. She knew how important this opportunity was going to be.

In spite of her own fears and in spite of the reservations of the station brass, things went down very smoothly on *People Are Talking*. From the beginning, everything seemed to fall into place. The low-key conversation, the interest that Oprah had in people generally, her ease and her professionalism. . . .

They had demoted her to get her out of the way while they tried to figure out how to break her contract. Now that she was on the shelf, they felt safe. And, oddly enough, for some reason, everything began to come together for Oprah Winfrey.

The show *worked*.

"I did this talk show," Oprah said. "I think I was interviewing some of the cast from *All My Children* and maybe the Carvel ice-cream man—really big-time stuff, you know!—but I'm telling you, I finished that show, and the minute it was over, I thought, 'Thank God! This is *it*. I've found out what I was *meant* to do. This is what I was *born for*. This is like *breathing*!' "

From the start, she worked well with her co-host, Richard Sher. The two of them had the right chemistry—as opposed to her earlier stint on the news, where the chemistry was "wrong."

"Co-hosting is like being married," Oprah said. "I don't think you could have found a better team than Richard and me." There was a kind of outrageousness that surfaced in her now and then on the air. And that outrageousness gave the show its *flavor*.

"I never considered myself funny," Oprah admitted. "Richard was always the funny one. I was always the straight man."

Straight man or not, it was the impishness and the zaniness in her that made Sher even funnier than he would have been ordinarily.

Sherry Burns, her producer on the *People Are Talking* show, recalled the transition in Oprah when she switched from hard news to soft news.

"She had hard times when I worked with her in Baltimore," Burns, later at WPLG-TV, Miami, recalled. "She fumbled around and co-anchored the news before doing the talk show. She was very young and they put her on the air to co-anchor." Obviously, that was a mistake, Burns said.

On this new show, she became an entirely different personality. "She is a wonderful, wonderful person," Burns said. "Who she is on-camera is exactly what she is off-camera." That was one of her main charms. She was and is *the* communicator.

"She's the universal woman. She gets right past the black thing. She's a totally approachable, real, warm person."

From the first, Burns realized what she had in Oprah. And the station began to play it the way Burns saw it. The idea was that after the show, people who had watched it would run into someone else and immediately ask, "Hey, did you see Oprah today? Did you see who she had on, did you see what she was talking about?"

The point was, there was something in her manner and in her instincts that seemed to dream up the right questions to ask—and come up with these questions while in conversation with the interviewee!

The questions were not written out in advance for Oprah, Burns remembered. "She asks the questions that people want to ask, *really* want to ask."

That was the key to her success in Baltimore.

Even the television brass at WJZ-TV came to realize what they had when they switched Oprah from news to talk.

Alan Frank, then one of the program executives at WJZ-TV, admitted:

"Oprah has a personality that's big and real and her own. And that comes right through the screen. She's very natural and people see that and they *like* it."

Although it came about so swiftly that Oprah hardly had the time to think about it, she did know that things had changed forever for her. She had co-anchored and she had co-newscast, but now that she was a co-hostess with a co-host, it was quite different.

"I was a restrained self," she said—at least at first. "The thing about being a co-host on a show is that it's like being married. And in ninety-nine out of a hundred cases in talk shows, the female is the one who gives."

But it did not seem to hurt her to give in Baltimore. She *loved* the feeling the show gave her.

"I felt as if I had come home," she recalled, talking about the switch from hard news to soft talk. "Doing talk shows is like breathing to me. Sometimes I think I am more comfortable in front of the camera than off. Plus, I have always had a hands-on experience with the audience."

The trauma of her permanent wave and the trauma of her voice lessons and the trauma of her failure as a newscaster were not the only down spots during those days in Baltimore. While her professional life was on the upgrade, her personal life was definitely on the downgrade.

The trouble, as it usually was, was with the men in her life—with Oprah's relationships with the opposite sex.

Looking back on it now, Oprah cannot actually understand why her sex life should have caused her such grief at that time.

Consider: Here she was, in her late twenties, on television, and making a six-figure salary that would have staggered her even a year before!

"I had so much going for me, but I still thought I was nothing without a man." The same thing she had thought when she was running after William Taylor when she was in college!

Part of Oprah's problem with men stemmed from the fact that she did not believe in living with a man unless she was married to him. Obviously, this idea must have been directly assimilated from the ideas of her father, Vernon Winfrey. It had little to do with Oprah's peer group and the ideas of that peer group. It was fashionable at the time to live with the opposite sex without benefit of clergy.

Yes. The idea of marrying a man before living with him was an old-fashioned idea at the time. It still is, really. Yet Oprah, for all her modern ideas and the things she had gone through in her rather short life up to that time, was not one to change her ideas about morality the way she would change a pair of shoes.

Although she's never wanted to discuss the details of the situation that gave her the most disturbing emotional problems of her life, she has spoken about Baltimore:

"I'd had a relationship with a man for four years. I wasn't living with him—I'd never lived with anyone—and I thought I was worthless without him."

The details were never forthcoming. Apparently this man continued to play the cat-and-mouse game with her —coming on to her, then running off, then outright spurning her.

"The more he rejected me," Oprah admitted, "the more I wanted him. I felt depleted, powerless."

It was much more than powerlessness that she felt. His actions absolutely bowled her over. She was unable to cope with herself because of her emotional involvement with him.

"Once I stayed in bed for three days, missing work," Oprah recalled, still puzzled at the hold the man had over her.

She was so down that she could not get herself up again. She seemed incapable of running her own life without this man, on whom she had placed so much of her dreams of the future.

Then came the final indignity.

Her lover provoked a knock-down, drag-out fight—probably with calculated deliberation. At the end of it, Oprah was stunned and unbelieving when he told her in no uncertain terms that he was through with her forever.

What she did next humiliates her to this day.

"I have been down on the floor on my knees groveling," she says. She remembers pleading with him, with this person who had done the best he could to ruin her life forever.

"Oh, God," she said, "why do we do this to ourselves?"

At first she thought he was simply threatening her, as he had done before. She thought he would be back, all forgiving and friendly once again. But as the days passed into weeks, she realized in her depressed state that he would not be back, ever.

It was at that time that Oprah Winfrey contemplated

suicide. "I don't think I was *really* serious about suicide," she said later. But, nevertheless, she did write a note to her best friend and confidante, telling her what she was going to do.

"It was a Saturday, around eight-thirty," Oprah recalled. "I'd been down on the floor, crying."

In the note to her friend, Oprah told her where all her insurance policies and papers were located. She even asked her friend to make sure that her plants were watered and cared for.

Later on Oprah found that note packed away; her friend had returned it to her to do with what she wished.

"I came across the note just lately," she told a magazine writer doing a story on her. "This is the first time I've talked about it. And I cried for the woman I was then."

Suicide was not Oprah's thing, really. She thought about those bad days later and analyzed herself.

"That suicide note has been much overplayed. I was never considering killing myself. I couldn't kill myself. I don't have the courage. I would be afraid that the minute I did it, something really good would happen, and I'd miss it!"

Nevertheless, she was still angry at the man who had caused her so much humiliation and rage—who had made her get down on the floor and grovel for him!

"There's nothing worse than rejection," she said. "It's worse than death. I would wish sometimes for the guy to die, because at least then I could deal with that. I could go to the grave and visit."

Her suicidal impulse did not return. She was, however, definitely in a depressed state of mind for days and weeks after that breakup. Professionally, she was doing well; personally, her life was hell.

"I was so adamant about being my own person that I wouldn't go for counseling."

She had always fought her own battles; she had always

been her own person. It never occurred to her that there might be something of an emotional nature that she would not be able to handle.

"Then it came to me. I realized there was no difference between me and an abused woman who has to go to a shelter—except that I could stay home. It was emotional abuse, which happens to women who stay in relationships that do not allow them to be all that they can be. You're not getting knocked around physically, but in terms of your ability to soar, your wings are clipped."

She was working out all these difficult psychological and personal matters in her mind herself, without the benefit of counsel.

"Women have that common bond when it comes to giving up power. I speak to a lot of women now, trying to get them to understand that each of us is responsible for herself. You can read that in books, but it isn't until you come to a spiritual understanding of who you are—not necessarily a religious feeling, but deep down, the spirit within—that you begin to take control."

Although she had never really continued with her church affiliation, it was obvious that Oprah had not strayed far in a psychological and spiritual sense from its protective shelter.

But the key fact she discovered in her soul-searching was that she had made a big mistake in dealing with this one man.

"I had given this man the power over my life. And I will never, never—as long as I'm black!—I will never give up my power to another person."

And what about that man now?

"Now I'm free!" she said. "And the man who caused me so much pain now says, 'I want to marry you.' " Oprah laughed. "And I say, 'Who doesn't?' "

Once she'd surfaced from that emotional plunge, Oprah felt ready to move on. "Getting out of that relationship was a major turning point, and the other turning point was *realizing* that getting out was a turning point," she said.

"As soon as I was able to put that relationship in its place, as soon as I was able to stop demeaning myself, things began to open up. I saw the light."

She began to understand more about herself. "I had *enjoyed* the pain. And I was as pained as any human being could be, I think. I realized I was like every battered woman I'd ever talked to. The only difference was that I didn't get hit physically. But it was the same mentality—believing I was *nothing* without this man."

Oprah Winfrey was coming to terms with herself in more ways than one in Baltimore. As she continued to find herself in a day-to-day fashion while she was performing on *People Are Talking*, she was coincidentally refashioning herself into the real Oprah Winfrey—the one who never before had existed!

In discovering others and what made them tick, Oprah was discovering things about herself—things that she had never before been aware of. She also found that her greatest gift was her ability to be Oprah Winfrey at all times.

What caused this blossoming and blooming of the real Oprah Winfrey was a combination of circumstances over which she had absolutely no control. Luck? Destiny? Fate? Who knows?

The format of the talk show had evolved into a much more complex and evocative form during the decades of the sixties and seventies. By the time Oprah was demoted to the Baltimore talk show *People Are Talking*, Phil Donahue had stepped down into the audience to bring each member of it into the magical aura of direct communication.

This suited Oprah Winfrey fine.

She had always been a hands-on person. She loved to talk directly to people on a friendly, communicating basis. And as she blossomed in the talk-show format in Baltimore,

Arthur Shay, Click/Chicago

Arthur Shay, Click/Chicago

Whether it's warmth or controversy, Oprah always draws an emotional response from her studio audience.

AP/Wide World Photos

Dana Fineman—Sygma

With Whoopie Goldberg

AP/Wide World Photos

At the wedding of Maria Shriver and Arnold Schwarzenegger, in Hyannis, Massachusetts

P/Wide World Photos

Willard Pugh as Harpo and Oprah as Sofia are married with their child in her arms in this scene from the Warner Bros. production *The Color Purple,* based on Alice Walker's novel.

Oprah photographed by Gordon Parks as Sofia, who fights every obstacle that stands in her path in *The Color Purple*

AP/Wide World Photos

A priceless look of delight after Oprah learns of her Oscar nomination for best supporting actress for her very first movie role in *The Color Purple*

Oprah joins Roger King (left), chairman of the board of King World, at a news conference to announce the national syndication of *The Oprah Winfrey Show*.

Arthur Shay, Click/Chicago

Oprah enjoys a rare moment of quiet in her office.

Arthur Shay, Click/Chicago

Every passerby is a fan when you're the hottest new celebrity in America!

she became even more a communicator and lightning rod for the television audience out there watching on their sets.

Also, instinctively, she was an actress. Not for her the constricted newscast, the small item to announce, the key word or phrase that spelled out the evening's news. It was always of interest to her how *she* came over, how *she* portrayed the dialogue, how *she* felt—not the audience.

With hard news, Oprah had frozen up. For then she was nothing more than a reader of wire-service material —the "rip-and-reads." Oprah did not fit into this category. She wanted time and expansiveness and thought.

Mostly she shone because she could communicate with another person one-on-one, at the same time communicating in a larger sense with the entire audience watching "out there."

"You have to allow enough of yourself to come through so that people see you as a person, not as a broadcaster," she once said. "Vulnerability is the key. Those two seconds after an interview ends, when the camera pans the set for a two-second close, are crucial. You have to keep going on with a guest, not ignore him or her. And you have to tell what went on during the commercial break. People want to know. They want you to be human."

Vulnerability became one of her key character elements. It was through her own special vulnerability, through her own sensitivity about people and things, that the viewing audience came to experience the lives and stories of the people with whom Oprah chatted.

And she knew she had to be tolerant. She had to be natural. She had to be somewhat ordinary so she would not frighten people away from her.

"I have a great sense of heritage," she said. "I feel a strong sense of legacy. But I'm not a flag-waving activist. I think excellence is the deterrent to racism. It's tough to convince others of that. I wanted to be part of the brother-sister network. I wanted to be nice, to be liked. If I thought somebody didn't like me, I was shattered."

And there, of course, lay her own special vulnerability. And that was not necessarily a drawback. In most cases it proved to be a real plus.

In the same way that a newspaper columnist differs from a hard-news writer, Oprah Winfrey became increasingly different from the news reporters at the station. And in the same way the columnist is able to control the subject of the day's piece by directing the material to specifics, Oprah could also control her own thoughts and emotions in dealing with whomever she was interviewing.

Part of her charisma, of course, was attributed to her blackness, particularly in the black-is-beautiful era, when serious attempts were being made to use blacks in prominent spots—like newscasting, like talk shows.

But in Oprah the Baltimore station had a nugget of pure gold. Not only was she visible and black and interesting—but she was primarily and fundamentally *intelligent.* More than intelligent, she was sharp and quick. Sharp and quick made her off-the-cuff remarks all the more memorable and quotable.

"I reached the point where I said whatever was on my mind. I approached the show as a surrogate viewer. What could a viewer ask next? I went with the flow of the conversation, instead of analyzing where I *wanted* to go. I loved to be surprised on the air."

One writer wrote about her success on *People Are Talking* in this way:

"She developed such a tangible rapport with her audience and guests that people were indeed talking."

And as the day-to-day routine on the Baltimore station continued, Oprah began to shed her own anonymity as a newscaster—which she had cultivated as news co-anchor—and became more and more Oprah in action and *only* Oprah in action.

"I'm a natural interviewer," Oprah has said. "I don't do a lot of preparation. I don't like to work from a script. It confuses me. I'm best when I can sit down, have a conversation, and develop some sort of insight."

Her strength was always her ability to wade right in, take charge of a conversation, and shape it as it came out, supercharge it with her own energy, and wing it. This was all coming over in her shows in Baltimore after she got going as the real Oprah Winfrey.

As she improved, Oprah began searching for more interesting conversationalists to balance her own tendency to probe. For example, the Carvel ice-cream man was an interesting subject for an interview, of course, but there might be people a lot more exciting to the viewers.

She began to shape her shows more deliberately. She knew that her interviews struck more sparks when she took on someone who was slightly controversial. That did not mean that she was waging some kind of internecine warfare with bigots or right-wingers, or even with people of a different political bias than hers—but it did mean that she wanted to take on people who were vigorous defenders of their own particular ideologies or philosophies.

She tried it once or twice at first just for fun. And when she came to see how well it worked—after all, Baltimore was a cosmopolitan area even though it was an old one with historical tradition and that kind of thing—she knew it would work anywhere in America.

And so she continued to send tapes of her broadcasts around to big-time places. She was having a ball in Baltimore, but there was probably more fun out there closer to the big time, maybe even—hey!—*in* the big time.

To hone her image for controversy, she tried all sorts of different subjects. She discussed divorce with divorcées and with people who did not believe in divorce. She talked about child rearing with people who had to work but didn't have the money to hire a nanny. She talked about the problems of Siamese twins joined at the head. Nothing was too difficult or too controversial for her.

And at the same time, of course, she talked to ordinary people who had their own very important problems—just getting along in life from day to day. People who were just like Oprah herself.

Nevertheless, Oprah was restless. She felt that it was time to be going somewhere else, preferably in an upward direction.

Sooner or later it might really happen—if she was lucky.

"I really grew up there in Baltimore, you understand," she said. "I felt natural and cared for there. But it was time to move on. I made a deliberate choice about where to go. Los Angeles? I'm black and female and they don't work in L.A. Orientals and Hispanics are their minorities. New York? I don't like New York, period. Washington? There are thirteen women to every man in D.C. Forget it. I have enough problems."

That left one obvious place—the third-largest television market in the country. It was "a big little town, sort of cosmopolitan country. The energy was different there than in Baltimore. It was more like New York, but you weren't overwhelmed like in New York."

Its name?

Chicago. That toddling town.

Helping Oprah on the *People Are Talking* show was a staff of resourceful and energetic people. One of them had became a fast friend of Oprah's. Debra DiMaio was the associate producer of the show. DiMaio worked with the producer, Sherry Burns, and several others to dream up ideas for the interviews Oprah had, and to go out and get interesting people for her to strike sparks off of.

Meanwhile, things were not standing still in the broadcasting business. People were moving around, as they always did, in the musical-chairs fashion familiar to anyone in the trade. It came Debbie DiMaio's time to feel restless too. She began hunting around for a job where she could be a full producer rather than just an associate.

She knew the value of the Oprah Winfrey interviews she had set up, and tapes of these went immediately into her portfolio. She began knocking on doors in New York, Los Angeles, and even Chicago—the home of the talk-show giant, Phil Donahue.

The revolving doors in the television business were moving even as she was being interviewed. In Chicago, WLS-TV, the ABC-TV affiliate, lost a co-producer on a morning talk show titled *A.M. Chicago*. Dennis Swanson, the station's general manager, began a hasty search for a replacement, and interviewed Debbie DiMaio. He noticed Oprah Winfrey and her freewheeling guest spots among the producer's tapes. He saw what kind of a person she was—certainly "dynamic," in his own words. He decided he would like to meet her sometime.

Debbie was lucky. She got the job on WLS-TV, and gave her notice to WJZ-TV in Baltimore. She then said her tearful good-byes to her associates there—including Oprah—and packed up to leave for Chicago.

Even before she began her new job, Robb Weller, the host of the show she had been hired to co-produce, suddenly was tapped for the big time and gave *his* notice to Swanson. Weller was headed for New York. Swanson was forced to begin a new talent hunt—this time for a host for the show.

The station manager had not forgotten Oprah Winfrey. Nor had Debbie DiMaio. Swanson borrowed her tapes and once again studied her work. In a few weeks, he had her in for an interview. There were other hosts and hostesses he saw—all of them good. But none, really, had the fire and the temperament that Oprah Winfrey had.

Still, Swanson knew it was a risk. Chicago was a complex community. He decided to go to the books to study her numbers in Baltimore. To his astonishment he found that in the past few months, Oprah Winfrey and *People Are Talking* had been *outscoring* the Phil Donahue talk show in Baltimore!

Of course, the *Donahue* show broadcast at the same time *People Are Talking* did; it emanated from Chicago. Swanson wondered if he might be able to pit Winfrey against Donahue and come out a winner in Chicago. It was a long shot, but just maybe . . .

And so Swanson *did* take the chance. He telephoned her and, with his fingers crossed, gave her the good news—that the station had decided to hire her for *A.M. Chicago.*

When she heard it, she told the people on the show in Baltimore where she was headed. This proposal was greeted with a great deal of skepticism.

"Don't go to that place!" one of her bosses told her. "They'll be marching down Michigan Avenue with signs!"

Oprah thought about that awhile, but finally scoffed it off. "So what?" she responded. "I'm going to go there and do the best I can."

And so Oprah Winfrey was hired to replace the departed Robb Weller. She would be the hostess of the early-morning talk show *A.M. Chicago.*

At more money. *Much* more money. She did very well indeed in *that* department. What she got was:

- a shade more than $200,000 a year in salary
- a four-year, unbreakable contract

Wow!

Oprah Winfrey packed up her bags, said good-bye to six years of fun—and frustration—and headed for Chicago. From that moment on, she never looked back.

8
A.M. Chicago

She arrived in Chicago not at all like the all-conquering heroine, but simply like herself—brassy, somewhat sassy, and at the same time vulnerable in that peculiarly aggressive Oprah Winfrey way.

Remembering her comeuppance in Nashville and then in Baltimore, where she had in both instances discovered shortcomings, she approached her new job with some diffidence. There was, of course, that overriding confidence that made her particular brand of diffidence *resemble* something quite like overconfidence.

She was, as usual, a study in opposites and contradictions. She felt that she had been set free. "I was released into the universe!" she described the feeling. And yet, she wondered—how free? What were the strictures of the job? Of the environment?

Like any wise employee, she took a good, long, appraising look at the show that she was going to hostess before she strode into the studio to take over, if indeed that was the way she would decide to play it.

"I sat down in my hotel room and watched the show,"

Oprah said later. "I'd never seen it before. I thought, 'Listen! Not good! Too frivolous!' "

She knew she was best at peaks and valleys—not at monotony. She liked to combine sexual surrogates one day with Donny and Marie Osmond the next. Then maybe the Ku Klux Klan, or perhaps female impersonators, or victims of incest.

And so even before she got there, she knew she would have to impress her own style on the show to make it over into something that would fit her snugly. But she was thankful that general manager Dennis Swanson had given her almost carte blanche to do what she would with the third-place, somewhat ailing *A.M. Chicago*.

After all, there had been a long series of talk-show hosts who had taken a stab at making the show a viable commodity. There was Robb Weller, her immediate predecessor. But there were also Sandi Freeman, Charlie Rose, and Steve Edwards. She had read the clips about them. They were all nice, talented professionals in the talk-show genre, who had come and gone, as *Chicago Tribune* reporter Cheryl Lavin put it, "without making a ripple."

The formula mix each of them had utilized had been simple enough—a little chitchat, a little fashion, a little personality stuff, a little cooking, a little homemaking. The idea implicit in their approach to the program was not to make waves—or ripples, as Lavin had said. And, in trying to avoid making waves, they had succeeded admirably in not making any progress in ratings either.

What struck Oprah as she studied the past reviews of the show was that the plan had apparently been to stay out of the way of the Phil Donahue juggernaut—the show had the same time slot, 9 A.M.—on another network. Nobody wanted to be in the rowboat when it was sliced in two by the ocean liner.

Whether that was what *really* obsessed the talk-show hosts

in the morning or not, Oprah vowed not to cower in the shadow of Donahue. She knew all about him. But she had outwitted him and outdrawn him in Baltimore. Perhaps it was a freak situation. But in spite of the fact that he was Número Uno in the talk-show business, she *had* outperformed him in her last job.

She had, in effect, outperformed the inventor of the format—the man who had gone out into the audience and made the morning yackety-yak format a living, viable communications thing. He was the reason people tuned in. He had, indeed, established the audience itself.

And the Lady from Baltimore had a good idea about that audience out there watching. It was, exactly the way Phil Donahue's was, predominantly the white housewife.

"She's out there, putting the laundry in," was the way Oprah phrased it. "Sometimes I'll just say, 'Hold on, I'm trying to get your attention. I know you just took the roast beef out and you're trying to thaw it out.' I'm really fascinated by what people *do* in their lives all day. I could have a discussion all day with just a housewife, saying, 'What do you do?' "

Actually, Oprah would be the first to admit that never in her life could she exist as a simple housewife.

"I'm not organized enough. I never made a bed. I figure I'll be back in it in twelve hours, so what's the point?"

But she knew something about her viewers too. She knew that though she herself could never be a housewife, they still considered her one of them—skin color notwithstanding.

The truth was, of course, otherwise. "I'm *not* one of them. I say to them, 'I could not do what you do.' I can't bake a roast. I have not been in a grocery store for two years. The last time I went grocery shopping, I went on a fresh-vegetable kick. I spent sixty-three dollars on fresh vegetables. I looked into the refrigerator one day and nearly died. I saw broccoli in there that had hair all over it and was moving. I called security for help."

All her meals were eaten out in restaurants, with the possible exception of an occasional fling at microwave popcorn.

But what she knew she had in common with her housewife viewers was "a belief system we all share in. I'm really no different from all of those women who are watching because I want the same things for my life that they want. I want to be happy, a sense of fulfillment, children who love me, respect from my husband."

Her gift, as she put it then, was in simply being able to "schmooze." *Schmooze* is a Yiddish word that means to indulge in small talk, chitchat, the exchange of inconsequential intimacies.

"I feel embraced by the camera. Like I'm doing exactly what I should be doing."

She must have been doing something right. The odds against her when she took on the Chicago market were formidable. During her stint in Baltimore, Oprah had gained a great deal of weight—a result of worrying about her job and how she was doing it. By the time she made the move to Chicago, she weighed about 180 pounds. At a height of five feet six inches, she packed it in as best she could.

"Everybody kept telling me that it was going to be impossible to succeed because I was going into Phil Donahue's hometown. So, you know, I'd eat and eat. I'd eat out of the nervousness of it all."

Television is a funny medium. It actually *enlarges* people—particularly those who are big to begin with. With Oprah, it put pounds on the pounds she already had.

Plus, of course, she was black.

But even if she seemed to dominate the picture tube and came right out into the room with the viewer, she didn't do badly at all. She loved to talk—to schmooze—and that was what she did at 9:00 every morning in Chicago.

The carefully developed down-home style that she had fabricated in her years in Baltimore and Nashville was somewhat of a surprise to native Chicagoans at first, but quite soon they got used to it. In fact, it added just a little edge to Oprah's image. Within a few weeks she was—surprise!—outdistancing the most famous television celebrity in town, Phil Donahue.

And on his own turf!

But—man!—was it cold in that town when she got there! A few days after she unpacked, the thermometer plunged to 27 degrees *below* zero. That was just a bit too much!

"This cold was awesome," she remarked. "It was *serious* cold. I thought I was delirious in the streets! I tell you, Negroes weren't built for this kind of weather! We start praying for the Motherland!"

But she survived. And in very good shape. Maybe the cold stimulated her, got the adrenaline flowing. Whatever, six weeks after she had begun doing *A.M. Chicago* the Nielsens showed her *ahead* of her competition. In the middle of March she was drawing 265,000 viewers, to 147,230 for Donahue. Not at all bad for a complete newcomer to the Windy City—after only twelve weeks' exposure!

And for some reason the critics liked her as much as the viewers did—a phenomenon not always enjoyed by popular personalities. Let's not say *liked*, let's say *loved.*

More important, the men at the station itself took her measure quickly and their immediate reaction was positive.

Program director Tim Bennett said, "She is a consummate communicator who is comfortable with what she's doing." He felt it was her capacity to reach people "out there" that made her so special. "She has an incredible entertainment range. She cuts right through the screen."

She might not have been good at reading the news and anchoring the hard stuff, but she was tops at the art of conversation.

"Oprah has this honesty with her audience and her guests that comes through," said Joe Ahern, the station manager. "No matter who you talk to—black, white, rich, poor, male, female, fat, thin—they say, 'You know, she's just like me.' "

Identification! That was the key.

Jon Anderson of the *Chicago Tribune* wrote of her: "On- and off-screen, her presence is undeniable, despite her short Chicago track record: three months. She is greeted by strangers on the street, recognized in restaurants and once was driven to work by a policeman when she was late and couldn't get a cab. Done live five days a week, her show waits for no person."

According to the reviewer for the *Chicago Sun-Times*, Lloyd Sachs, Phil Donahue "is so sincere, he becomes insincerer. Oprah's a freer spirit."

Much of the "freer spirit" probably came from Oprah's deeply ingrained work habits.

"I usually *don't* do any homework," she admitted. "I really have learned that for me and my style of interviewing, the less preparation I do, the better—because what everybody is now calling Oprah's success is me being spontaneous, and that's all it is."

But spontaneity sometimes brought some heat. Sometimes plenty of heat. And Oprah kept that thought in her mind at all times too.

"If things go bad, it's *my* buns out there."

Generally speaking, Oprah did not appear to the reviewers as tough as Donahue. While Donahue might be trying to winkle out the truth about the morality of a porn queen, Oprah would just ask the porn queen something like: "Don't you get sore?"

Besides that, Sachs pointed out, Donahue would never kick off his shoes in the middle of the show and tell all his viewers, "My feet are killing me."

Fran Preston, a spokesperson at WLS-TV, put it in perspective when she wrote: "If a gorgeous blue-eyed blonde says she's having troubles, you don't believe her. Oprah, you believe. She isn't threatening."

It was a highly competitive situation, with plenty of heat on both Oprah and Donahue. Oprah kept that salient point in her mind at all times.

Her intuition was a formidable element of her personality—especially in understanding exactly what kind of guests would pull in the most viewers. And she handled those guests like a consummate pro—getting the best out of each of them *without any advance study.*

Watching her show was similar to watching an ad-lib session among seasoned veterans of the vaudeville or music-hall circuit.

For example:

The actor Dudley Moore was talking about his personal life, particularly his sex life. Oprah noted that Moore's companions were quite frequently taller than him; that wouldn't be strange, inasmuch as Moore was shorter than average.

Now Oprah came to the question that she said was *the* question she had always wondered about.

"Aren't there some technical problems posed by your habit of always wanting to sleep with taller women?"

Moore thought a moment.

"Well," he replied slowly, "most of their length seems to be in their legs. Luckily."

When Oprah got Boy George on the show, she got him to talk about his habit of appearing in women's clothes. And then came the typical Oprah-like question—one she said she had always wondered about.

"What does your *mother* think when you go out?"

Boy George frowned. "She says she never thought she'd be proud to have a son dressed up like a transvestite."

On one occasion Oprah was interviewing a woman who was describing a bizarre situation in which she was seduced by seven priests in succession.

After the audience had managed to absorb this information, Oprah got right at the question that had been bothering her.

"What did you *do* when the first one pulled his pants down?" she asked.

"Nothing," the woman responded. There was a long pause. "And then he took my hand."

It was not only sex that engaged the viewers. She was talking one day with James Coco, chatting about this and that, until they got around to diets and weight control. Coco had gone on a stringent diet and had lost a hundred pounds.

A hundred pounds!

"See," said Oprah seriously, "God was looking out for you." Then, with a mischievous glint in her eye: "Sometimes She does."

She was once engaged in a serious discussion with a female scientist about the size of the penis, in particular about the difference it made in a satisfactory sexual encounter. Did the size of the penis, in effect, have anything to do with the degree of female satisfaction?

The discussion did not seem to be getting to the point that Oprah was interested in.

"If you had your choice, you'd like to have a big one if you could! Right? Bring a big one home to Mama!"

(NOTE: This one is always listed as a starred item in any collection of Oprah-isms.)

She was interviewing actress Sally Field at one time and the talk turned to Burt Reynolds, with whom the actress was involved and also had made several very funny films.

Oprah was thinking about the actor, and a sudden thought occurred to her.

"Does Burt sleep with his toupee on or off?"

Sally Field froze. "I . . . beg . . . your . . . pardon."

Oprah simply shifted gears and pulled another question down off the wall of her subconscious—and the show went on.

Then there was the time she brought a group of nudists on the show as guests. They appeared in their native garb—the emperor's clothes.

Even Oprah had to think twice about that show. It was one of the few that she admitted made her nervous.

"We had these nudists on—I mean actual *naked* people. I pride myself in being real honest, but on this show I was really *faking* it. I had to act like it was a perfectly normal thing to be interviewing a bunch of naked people—and *not* look. I wanted to look straight into the camera and announce, 'My God! There are penises here!' "

(NOTE FOR THE PRUDENT: The on-air broadcast only showed head-and-shoulders shots.)

A visiting sociologist was once describing a situation in which two female roommates who were just good friends suddenly evolved virtually overnight into a lesbian couple. Each step brought gasps from the audience.

Oprah's eyes opened wide as the sociologist continued, until finally she sighed and cried out:

"I'm *never* getting a roommate!"

She even brought up an interesting problem in a serious discussion about television commercials. The talk turned to the kinds of commercials made for Calvin Klein clothes.

Finally Oprah burst out with her thoughts:

"I hate *all* those jeans ads. They all have such tiny little butts in those ads!"

She interviewed a woman named "Vicky" who had been unable to achieve orgasm after eighteen years of marriage. Going to a counselor, she had been introduced to a male sex surrogate who had given her lessons.

"Would you like to tell us what it was like for you, Vicky, when you had your first orgasm?" Oprah asked the woman matter-of-factly.

"May I be explicit?" the woman asked.

Of course, Oprah nodded.

"Well, he started by using his finger, very gently, inside me. I felt a slight contraction—"

At that point one of the stagehands groaned and buried her face in her hands, while the stage manager rushed out of his booth, making frantic signs to Oprah to "wrap" the segment.

Oprah turned quickly, and said smartly: "Thank you very much. Now we'll take a break."

While the commercial rolled, Oprah swung around in the aisle to face the audience with a mock smile. "When she said 'explicit,' I didn't mean *that* explicit! Jesus Christ! Did I hold my face right?"

The audience whooped.

Oprah waved her hands. "Now the boss is downstairs screaming." She turned to Vicky with a sigh. "So much for telling the truth. Lie a little!"

She was working on the show twenty-four hours of every day. If she was not reading newspapers and magazines for ideas, she was *rehearsing*. This item appeared one day tucked away in a Chicago gossip column:

> QUESTION: Who was that blindfolded woman eating dinner at Yvette's the other night?

ANSWER: It was *A.M. Chicago*'s Oprah Winfrey, working on a special show about the problems of the visually handicapped. Just part of her "blind day."

Although Oprah took her success pretty much in stride, almost as if she had always thought that she would be a big hit on television, she had the ability to analyze herself—warts and all.

"My greatest gift is my ability to be myself at all times, no matter what," she said once. "I am as comfortable in front of the camera with a million people watching me as I am sitting here talking to you. I have the ability to be perfectly vulnerable at all times."

And that agreed pretty closely with what her own producer, Debbie DiMaio, said about her. "She's one hundred percent the same off-camera as on. People like her because they can relate to her. She's got all the same problems—overweight, boyfriend troubles, she's been poor. So when people see her on television they can say, 'That's my friend Oprah.' "

And they did. They would wave at her from buses, or run up to her on the street to hug her. When they did, she hugged them right back.

Dennis Swanson, the man who hired her for the job, said that he had selected her out of a long list of strong candidates for one special reason only.

"She was the best—and I wanted the best." When he got her, he got bonuses too, he said. "She is the same person on-camera as she is off-camera. She's a bundle of energy and fun to be around." And it rubbed off on the audience at the studio, the people on the telephones, and the others watching and listening "out there."

Nor did she really lay her popularity to the fact that she was a beautiful black in an era when black was still beautiful.

"I transcend race, really. I believe that I have a higher

calling. What I do goes beyond the realm of everyday parameters. I am profoundly effective. I know people really, really *love* me, *love* me, *love* me. A bonding of the human spirit takes place. Being able to lift a whole consciousness—that's what I do."

And as for all the money she was making, "I can assure you that people who think accomplishment has gone to my head are the very people who, if it were happening to them, would have been blown out of the water. I don't want to be portrayed as someone who's gotten a little money and has gone bonkers over it. I still haven't jumped up and down about becoming a millionaire. *Money* doesn't define me."

No, money did *not* define her. But she thought about it a lot—even now, after she had made it. "It's amazing to me that I get *paid* to be myself. This is the best time of my life, and I have sense enough to know it's the best. My dream is to continue being Oprah. She's a good ol' girl!"

After seven months in her morning time slot, the *A.M. Chicago* show was extended from a half hour to an hour. And by the end of 1984, Oprah Winfrey was definitely a phenomenon in Chicago—just as much a phenomenon as Phil Donahue had been before her, when he had become king of the talk shows. And now she was gobbling up a lot more of his 9:00 A.M. share of the market than she had when she was starting.

The rumors went out that she was making at least $200,000 a year—she was indeed—and there were other rumors that her salary would go up in 1985. It was making up for all the bad times before.

She broke into the national big time in December 1984 when *Newsweek* ran a page-long article on her. "About all that's missing for Chicago's hottest media star," the piece said, "is a national stage, but considering the city's extraordinary track record for helping launch network glitterati (among them: Dave Garroway, Jane Pauley, Frank Reynolds, John Chancellor, and Bill Kurtis), many in the industry believe that her ascent remains only a matter of time."

The prophecy was absolutely on the nose.

In January 1985 the *Donahue* show quite suddenly pulled up stakes, folded its tent, and took off for New York City. Of course the *real* reason was that Donahue and his second wife—actress-producer Marlo Thomas—wanted to spend more time together. She was appearing on Broadway and Donahue was working out of Chicago—their erratic schedule was interfering with their marriage.

Oprah was amused at the way it played. "It's just that here we are stomping him in the ratings, you know, and suddenly—he's gone! It was maahvelous!"

A farewell luncheon was held for Phil Donahue and his crew in January 1985. At the affair he was quite gracious to Oprah Winfrey, wishing her the best of luck—"but not in my time period."

Oprah was, as she put it—"thrilled . . . This was *Phil Donahue* talking about *me*!"

And shortly after that, he . . . split.

"Marlo, not me, made him move," Oprah knew. But still it did look—

Once Donahue had left his home turf, Oprah's possession of it increased in astronomical proportions. And she became more and more daring in her selection of guests.

On New Year's Day, 1985, she was sassy enough to book female members of the Ku Klux Klan for her show!

"I was reading the paper and I said, 'Let's get the Klan girls on.' " And she did.

The women appeared dressed in big white sheets and cone hats, just like their male counterparts. In the discussion that followed—interspersed with Oprah's acidulous comments—they maintained that it was stated in the Bible that the races of the world should be separate.

Oprah, with a gleam in her eye, invited them all to lunch with her. They declined.

Most of the audience was indignant at what they considered to be a slap in the face. "I would have slapped *them*!" one woman told Oprah.

Oprah shook her head and addressed the audience. "What you must understand is that when the show is over, those people are still going to be Klan girls, and I'm still going to be Oprah. You can only hope to expose racism for what it *is*."

By the time 1985 was under way, it was obvious that Oprah had hit her stride and simply could not be stopped. She began to assume even more control over production of the show than she had done previously. She became an avid reader of newspapers, magazines, and books. She wanted to know what was going on all over the world—everything that might become grist for the mill of her show. Even though the show was a local one, it was beginning to get national attention. She could get almost anyone on she wanted now.

She worked daily with her staff members, figuring out what would go and what would not go.

"Nothing gets booked if I don't want it," she said. "We are a team; but if I don't want to do it, it doesn't make sense to book it, because a lot depends on my interest and energy."

Those threats of national television turned out to be more than a simple gleam in a press agent's eye. Early in 1985, Oprah Winfrey "went national" when she appeared on somebody else's show. She was invited by Joan Rivers, who was substituting for Johnny Carson, to be a guest on *The Tonight Show*.

Rivers had heard about Oprah's popularity in Chicago, and wanted to see if it was justified. Oprah the overconfident was actually underconfident just before going to the

West Coast to appear. She said that she was so nervous she wouldn't even watch the Carson show for two weeks!

The upshot of the visit was very good press for Oprah and a publicized "duel" between Rivers and Oprah to see who could lose weight more successfully. Oprah said she would lose thirty pounds if Joan Rivers would lose five. "Six pounds for every one of yours!"

After talking about Oprah's early days on the pig farm, Rivers took her through the hard times in Milwaukee, her selection as Miss Fire Prevention in Nashville, and some of her weight-loss efforts in the past.

"How did you gain the weight?" Rivers asked, looking Oprah over critically.

"I ate."

"You're a pretty girl and single," Rivers shot back. "Lose it!"

"I'll lose it if you'll lose it," Oprah said.

And so the duel was on.

During her stay in Hollywood, Oprah took her technical crew with her to film some "location" spots for the Chicago show later on. She would be doing a show on ABC-TV's upcoming TV-movie *Hollywood Wives*. She had lunch at Ma Maison, visited all the Rodeo Drive shops with Mary Crosby and Angie Dickinson, and even chatted with Jackie Collins, the author of the novel *Hollywood Wives* and sister of *Dynasty*'s Joan Collins.

She renewed her longtime acquaintance with Maria Shriver, whom she had met in her Baltimore days when Shriver was working with *CBS Morning News*. The two had immediately hit it off, prompting Shriver to call Oprah "one of my closest friends."

Shriver was very taken with her: "She asks the questions people really want to know. She has no inhibitions. She doesn't worry about her image or her credibility. She just asks from her gut."

Along with Shriver in Hollywood was weight-lifting actor Arnold Schwarzenegger, he of the marvelous musculature, what the news media liked to tab "Shriver's longtime pal"—read *lover*.

Schwarzenegger kept needling Oprah. "Why do you gain weight?" the muscle-bound strongman kept asking. It was the same kind of thrust she had gotten from Joan Rivers. Who needed that from friends?

"I decided I was going to have a good time no matter what or who."

When Shriver and Schwarzenegger were married at the Kennedy compound on Cape Cod on April 26 the following year, Oprah attended as an invited guest of the bride—indeed, more than that. As she told a friend: "My dear, I was *in* it." She was going to recite from memory Elizabeth Barrett Browning's classic love sonnet "How Do I Love Thee?" but was petrified that she might blow a line. None other than Jacqueline Bouvier Kennedy Onassis advised her: "Why don't you just take it up and read it?"

"I figured if Jackie O. says I can read it, I'll read it."

And she did.

Oprah celebrated her thirty-first birthday on the 1985 Hollywood swing by dining at fashionable Spago's restaurant. *Then*, in February, she began her televised diet to knock off fifteen of the thirty pounds she had promised to Joan Rivers.

9
Life with Sofia

In 1985 Quincy Jones was a very busy man. A record producer—among singing stars he had guided to substantial success were such luminaries as Michael Jackson and Frank Sinatra—Jones was moving into the motion-picture business. Among the current properties he had on hold was the Alice Walker novel *The Color Purple*, a story in letter form about blacks growing up in the South. It had become a favorite among readers of all "colors" from the date of its publication.

Meanwhile, Jones was involved in a lawsuit against Michael Jackson—something about contractual obligations and money. There was a trial going on in Chicago, and Jones had been called to testify in court. A busy man, he had arranged a six-hour appearance, and booked a hotel room for a quick in and then a quick out.

Eating breakfast in his room, Jones switched the television on and glanced at it desultorily as he munched his toast and drank his coffee. At the time, he was beginning to assemble a number of musical pieces for the background of the script for *The Color Purple*, which had been made into a screenplay by Menno Meyjes.

It was mostly music that was on his mind, since he was responsible for that part of the picture. But he was also one of the film's producers, along with Steven Spielberg, Kathleen Kennedy, and Frank Marshall. As he glanced at the television screen he became aware of a peculiar phenomenon.

He was watching someone who could have stepped right out of the pages of Menno Meyjes's script *and* Alice Walker's book. He was gazing at Sofia.

This Sofia was working a program called *A.M. Chicago*. He continued to watch her, fascinated. She had the strength of Sofia, and the brass. And she was a powerful personality on the air. She filled the screen.

Minutes after the show had finished he had her name and was on the telephone to California. There he was connected with Reuben Cannon and Associates, which was handling casting for the upcoming picture.

Meanwhile, Oprah Winfrey was blissfully unaware of the wheels within wheels that were beginning to turn for her. She had read the book *The Color Purple* when it was first published.

"I'm the kind of person who reads all the papers on Sunday," she said, "so I had gone to get *The New York Times*—I was working in Baltimore at the time—and the first thing I pulled out of all the papers was the book review.

"I read this review of *The Color Purple,* and I went to the bookstore and said, 'Okay, the minute it comes in, call me.' " The store did and she read it immediately. It hit her like a ton of bricks. She was so pleased with it that she handed out copies to all her friends.

"It's all I talked about for two years."

Of course the character who interested her the most was Sofia, a woman who was spirited and strong, and who refused to let her spirit be broken—first by an abusive husband, and finally by prison authorities. She stood for what Oprah stood for herself—the indomitable spirit of the human being.

Even at that early date, Oprah had been sure that Hollywood would make the book into a movie—even if it was only a handful of letters written back and forth between members of a family.

Deep inside, of course, she was thinking to herself:

"Oh my God, please, please, somehow, somewhere, let me find a way to get in this movie. I'll do *anything*: be 'best boy,' a 'water girl.' "

Sure enough, in May 1985 the announcement appeared in the press that *The Color Purple* was soon going to go into production. But all Oprah did was think about it and hope and pray. She made no other move.

"I'm not the kind of person who could even go knock on doors and be turned down a lot, because I've been in television so long that my ego couldn't take it. That's why I did not become an actress."

The truth of the matter was she had been told that she could never be a star and that she would have to settle for reading the news or acting as a television talk-show hostess. *Because* she would not push for herself.

"You don't *want* to become an actress," one of her speech coaches had told her. "You want to be a *star*. You're not willing to come here [to New York] and wait on tables."

And Oprah had responded to this statement with the following: "Well, I guess not, because I'm already making substantial money as a television person, and it'd be hard for me to put all that down and go and wait on tables."

But inside, even then, she was thinking hard: "Well, one day, somehow, I know it's going to happen. I'll probably end up having to be discovered, because I certainly am not going to knock on doors."

And so she had reasoned out the way that she would become an actress, never really dreaming that it would actually happen that way. But behind-the-scenes things were happening right along those lines, and she was not aware of it. In effect, Oprah Winfrey was auditioning for the role of Sofia in *The Color Purple* without even knowing it.

"That's why it pays to be your best all the time," she concluded later, "because you never know who's watching." It might be Quincy Jones. Or Reuben Cannon himself. Or Steven Spielberg.

"I act as if everything depends upon me and pray as if everything depends upon God. Success in your work is not luck. If the door opens and you're not ready to go through . . . Acting, like poker, requires a great deal of skill, but you win or lose on how you apply good fortune."

As Aljean Harmetz once put it in *The New York Times*, "Miss Winfrey has always been ready to go through any door, and, if the door wouldn't open, she has talked it down."

One week after Jones had spotted Oprah in Chicago, the Reuben Cannon people contacted her officially, and Oprah was on her way to the West Coast to make a screen test for the role of Sofia.

Spielberg called her into the office after the tests had been made and run off on the screen. He told her the truth. She was ideal for the role of Sofia, but they would have to test other people for the part. After all, she was not an experienced actress.

And so she had to wait for the decision to be made.

It was not easy.

But meanwhile Oprah was involved in her "duel" with Joan Rivers. She found herself eating too heavily, and checked into a health farm to take off the pounds. It was while she was there, trying to lose weight without going crazy, that casting director Reuben Cannon telephoned her.

When he gave her the good news—that she would play

Sofia—she cheered and cheered. She would be svelte for Joan Rivers and she would also be playing Sofia!

"What are you doing at that health farm?" Cannon asked her after a short pause.

"Losing weight! I'm on a diet! I just lost thirty pounds! Congratulate me!"

Cannon snorted. "You're playing Sofia! You can't lose weight. Whatever you've lost, you'd better go out and find it again."

Torn between trying to get down to a workable figure for her television show and Joan Rivers, and trying to get up to a weight that would make her proper for Sofia, Oprah surrendered and gained poundage quickly for the role.

And that day, she said—the day she was told she had won the role of Sofia in the picture—"was the single happiest day of my life." She felt "blessed. . . . Quincy Jones became my Number One favorite person in the universe!"

The first people to know of her good luck were the seven people with whom she worked every day at the station.

Whoopi Goldberg won the role of Celie, the lead in the film. When Oprah finally met her, Goldberg confessed that she had always hungered for the part of Sofia.

"You have the one role I wanted," she told her.

The film was made during eight weeks of location work in South Carolina and in Hollywood for the looping and cutting. Oprah went into the job with her usual self-confidence—but actually she understood her shortcomings and her problems. She had never done anything like this before.

Although acting was instinctive to her from the day she was born—witness her dramatic ploys in Milwaukee to get herself a new pair of glasses, or make her puppy a hero—she knew she was not honestly a professional actress.

She thought: "What if I do my best and it's just not good enough?" And so she worked hard. Very hard. From the very first.

Actually, she need not have worried that much. Spielberg once commented to Joe Ahern, the station manager at WLS-TV: "When you turn the camera on Oprah, she speaks the truth."

He would have taken her no matter what she did.

"Everybody was a joy to work with," Oprah said of the film company later. "We were a family."

Every day the actors would watch the dailies and react to the performances. Whoopi Goldberg was the envy of everyone.

"*She* didn't even open her mouth!" Oprah said.

Overall, Oprah realized that in a motion picture, everyone there became part of a very special team.

"Everyone on the set, from the grip to the gaffer to Spielberg and the star, gave me positive energy."

There were, nevertheless, difficult moments for her.

"I kept a journal while we were shooting, and at the end of two weeks, I wrote that I would probably have to fake it."

What she meant was that she had been unable to get a handle on the role she was doing. "I felt I was never going to make it through to the end. I was devastated because Steven [Spielberg] had asked me to cry on cue and I couldn't do it. It was my first movie and I thought, an actress should be able to do that."

There were other problems.

"The cinematographer was complaining: 'She missed her light.' I thought to myself, not only do I have to stay in character, hit the mark, and hit the light, but I have to remember my lines!"

Things were happening all around her in the movie business too—and the uneasiness that permeated the industry began to find its way into her. It was at that time that Eric Stoltz was replaced by Michael J. Fox in *Back to the Future.* Naturally, all the actors were talking about it. Oprah was thinking: "That's me! I'm next."

And then came the moment she had mentioned in her journal. Spielberg wanted her to cry on cue.

"The day he asked me to cry—it's still the most humiliating day of my life. The scene, which—ironically—was omitted from the movie in the final cut, had Harpo [Sofia's husband in the movie] jump up on a table and make a wonderful speech about the juke joint being his place and me being his woman."

Spielberg came over to Oprah and asked her: "Do you think you can cry?"

Oprah put up a brash front. She told him she certainly could.

"Well, as it happened, they switched speeches. Harpo recited a sonnet instead of his speech, and I'm sitting there thinking, 'Oh my God, they're doing this so I can cry.' I still couldn't do it, so I started plucking my eyebrows and tried to stick them under my contact lenses."

Anything to get the tears to flow.

"After a whole day of this, I went home and cried all night because I couldn't cry on cue."

Her associates back in Chicago were very supportive of Oprah when she was in the Deep South on the film. They sent her weekly care packages and even went down in groups to visit her.

For Oprah, making the transition from talk-show hostess to motion-picture supporting actress was extremely difficult. "It was shocking," she said. "I was so concerned about being able to create a life that was real. I wondered how you were supposed to act out something that was real."

And, as in most cases, she got tips from the people with whom she was working. One important one came from the late Adolph Caesar, who played Mr.'s father in the film. Caesar, incidentally, was nominated for an Oscar for his role in *A Soldier's Story*.

Caesar's advice concerned the trick of "getting into a role." Oprah said, "He told me to give myself over to the character and let the character take control. He told me to pretend the character had a life beyond the screen."

That was extremely good advice. Oprah understood finally what he meant.

But before that happened, there was still the difficult matter of determining the character itself! What Oprah needed was a role model, in the sense of someone she could pretend to *be* while she played Sofia. The author of the book had visualized a certain person; naturally Oprah would *look* different. But somehow she must try to evoke the same image that Walker had when she wrote the character.

Finally Oprah hit on the proper person. It was Fannie Lou Hamer, a rural Mississippi civil rights leader in the 1960s. Oprah had read a great deal about her, and had been struck by the woman's forbearance in the face of brutalization and years spent in jail in the fight for civil rights.

"I had Fannie Lou Hamer in the back of my head," Oprah said. "I'm aware of my legacy [to Hamer], which is why I was honored to play Sofia. She was part of all those women I'd been carrying around inside me for years. In high school oratory contests, while everybody else did a speech from *Inherit the Wind*, I'd be doing something from Margaret Walker's *Jubilee,* about a slave woman after the Civil War, or Sojourner Truth's 'Ain't I a Woman?' speech."

Sure, Sofia was funny, and ferocious, tough, and powerful—but the role called for her reaction *after* she was degraded and battered. The real crux of the role was the fact that even after she had been stomped on and ground into the dirt she was still willing to talk in her own voice about where she stood and what she believed in.

The heroism of the role came out only at the *end* of the film.

That was the "big speech"—that was the evocative moment toward which the whole long role moved.

Oprah was forced to plumb the depths of her feelings to get that moment right during the eight-week shooting of the picture.

Everything hinged on that key scene at the dinner table, when Sofia, who had said little after her return from prison, finally came out with what was her major speech—and *the* key speech of the picture.

"I remember having sat there for three days of shooting, rocking at the table," Oprah recalled. "Mine was the last angle to be shot." In fact, it was the kernel of the whole dramatic episode—in effect, of the whole story. "I had been sitting there watching everybody else. I had a lot of time to think about the years Sofia spent in jail, and how thousands of women and men, all the people who marched in Selma, were thrown in jail and what those years must have been like.

"Sofia finally speaking was a victory for all of us, and for me." Yes, she was indeed Fannie Lou Hamer at that moment.

The speech set the picture on fire.

"It was a major breakthrough for me. . . . It was the day I became an actress."

Soon it was all over and she was back in Chicago doing her show under much less strain and torment. By the time she had finished filming, she had no idea at all if she had done a good job or a bad job in the part.

She waited for the film to come out to find out.

It was premiered in December 1985, and she was accompanied by her staff to New York. It was an instant hit, but the reviews weren't all that tremendously impressive. In its subhead, *Variety* noted: OVERPRODUCED, OVERLY MA-

NIPULATIVE STEVEN SPIELBERG DRAMA IS SAVED BY OUTSTANDING PERFORMANCES.

In a long review, *Variety* expressed the feeling that it could have been better. "There are some great scenes and great performances in *The Color Purple,*" it began, "but it is not a great film."

Spielberg was criticized for "overblown production" that tended to destroy the emotions created. "But the characters created in Alice Walker's novel are so vivid that even this doesn't kill them off and there is still much to applaud (and cry about) here."

In all, "Box-office outlook is promising without approaching other Spielberg super-hits."

For those who had not read the original Walker book, the review said, the picture would not prove a disappointment. But for those who had, it might leave something to be desired.

"Much of what is successful in the film is from the book." But, "Overall, the film lacks the depth, variety, and richness of the book."

Nevertheless, Oprah Winfrey came out very well. "Saving grace of the film are the performances," the *Variety* review stated. Among these standouts it listed "Oprah Winfrey's burly Sofia."

The New York Times was generally negative in its review of the picture, damning with faint praise. "Mr. Spielberg has looked on the sunny side of Miss Walker's novel, fashioning a grand, multi-hanky entertainment that is as pretty and lavish as the book is plain. . . .

"Some parts of it are rapturous and stirring, others hugely improbable, and the film moves unpredictably from one mode to another."

The film, generally, Janet Maslin wrote, is an "upbeat, affirmative fable in which optimism, patience, and family loyalty emerge as cardinal virtues, and in which even the wife-beating villain has charm."

She goes on: "Oprah Winfrey, as Celie's stepdaughter-in-law Sofia, has the most exaggeratedly comic role in the film, but she handles it gracefully. . . .

"One of the most unwieldy episodes in Miss Walker's book is similarly troublesome in the movie: it shows what happens after Sofia, having been sorely provoked, attacks a white woman who is the mayor's wife. Sofia goes to prison for long enough to see her health and her spirit broken, and when she emerges, she is hired by the mayor's wife as a servant. On Christmas day, Sofia's first chance to see her family in years, her employer plays Lady Bountiful and allows Sofia to drive home for the day, but fifteen minutes later Sofia is torn away from her relatives."

Writing in *The Washington Post,* Courtland Milloy related how he had come to the theater to pick the picture apart for the female-chauvinistic way it treated black men, but ended up by being "blindsided" by it.

"By the time Sofia (Oprah Winfrey) was released from prison and came home all swollen and beaten with that dead eye, I was emotionally drained. Not because of the pain on the screen, but because of that which had been revealed around me."

He referred to the weeping of the black women in the audience with him.

"Then Sofia's daughter came outside to greet her, but because the girl had not seen her mother in such a long time, she could not remember her. And when the little girl said ever so politely, 'Nice to meet you, ma'am,' I was a goner."

Not so Pauline Kael in *The New Yorker*. She felt that the picture had not caught the "joyous emotional swing" of the "inspirational passages" in the book—citing especially the one that gave the book its title:

Shug Avery, telling Celie about God and love, says: "It pisses God off if you walk by the color purple in a field somewhere and don't notice it."

The movie missed this particular diction, she wrote—the "raw, cadenced dialect, an artful version of a rural near-illiterate's black English" in which Walker had written the book.

She also complained that Menno Meyjes's script had not "reshaped the novel into a dramatic structure." And Spielberg, she hinted, seemed to have missed the main theme of the book: "the lyrical presentation of the healing power of love. He may not have understood this, because he approaches the material with undue timidity."

But the capper involved Oprah's acting:

"Except for the dimpled Oprah Winfrey as the powerhouse Sofia, whose mighty punch at a white man lands her in jail for twelve years, the performers don't make a very strong impression."

Other reviewers also selected Oprah among the peaks of a film that had both peaks and valleys.

David Ansen of *Newsweek* wrote: "Far flashier [than Whoopi Goldberg's Celie] is Oprah Winfrey's role as Sofia, the stout, belligerently proud wife of Mr.'s son Harpo (Willard Pugh), and a woman who pays dearly for her pride. As played by Winfrey, the Chicago talk-show host, she's a brazen delight."

Michael H. Seitz, in *The Progressive,* found the film itself watered down from the Alice Walker novel. The language was even "cleaned up," which disturbed Seitz. "By recasting the dialogue in somewhat closer to standard English, the movie loses much in linguistic color and authenticity."

But he did find the acting good. "The acting was generally quite stirring—especially that of Whoopi Goldberg as Celie and Oprah Winfrey as Sofia."

Stanley Kauffmann, in *The New Republic,* found the film unremarkable, but he did say:

"Two women are outstanding. Oprah Winfrey is a plump proud woman who pays grievously for her pride. Margaret

Avery is Shug (short for Sugar), the singer who bewitches Celie's husband."

David Sterritt, in *The Christian Science Monitor,* observed that Oprah Winfrey was "a revelation as a feisty woman with hardships as bad as Celie's."

Kenneth R. Hey, in *USA Today,* simply mentioned Oprah Winfrey in passing—"Harpo (Willard Pugh) marries Sofia (Oprah Winfrey), a brash independent woman who, even though she runs afoul of the white establishment, gives Celie her first glimpse of something other than the slavery she knows."

For Richard A. Blake in *America,* Spielberg made the film that should have been a search for survival and dignity in rural Georgia into a film of "grandeur" that was mismatched with the gritty, brutal story. Nevertheless, "As Sofia, the one black woman capable of fighting back against men and white people, Oprah Winfrey transforms a comic caricature into a living person."

Commonweal wrote that "Spielberg and his cast (Margaret Avery, Rae Dawn Chong, Oprah Winfrey, and Whoopi Goldberg as the heroine, Celie) make *The Color Purple* creditable and worthwhile."

In spite of the acceptance of the picture by many theatergoers, the film began to draw a number of negative responses—particularly from the black community.

"No, it is not just a movie," Nate Clay, the editor of *The Chicago Metro News,* said. "It is a statement made out of context used as a pretext to take one more lick at society's rejects."

Willis Edward, president of the Beverly Hills chapter of the National Association for the Advancement of Colored People, argued in an interview that the movie "never showed the good" about black men.

"This is not a 'black film,' " Oprah retorted at a special preview of the picture in Washington, D.C. "It's about endurance, survival, faith, and ultimate triumph. Whatever you want is in you."

At the film's premiere in Los Angeles on December 18, 1985, dozens of picketers marched outside the theater.

In Chicago, nearly a thousand blacks crammed into the Progressive Community Church for a heated discussion of the film.

More than two hundred people in New York filled the fellowship hall at St. James Presbyterian Church in Harlem for a similar exchange.

Lerone Bennett, a historian and senior editor of *Ebony* magazine, said of Spielberg: "He doesn't show us the strong black women who nursed the sick and cared for the orphans and organized clubs and, in general, exercised a leadership role denied white women by white society. What Steven Spielberg doesn't show us, in short, is the color black."

Vernon Jarrett, a *Chicago Sun-Times* columnist, wrote: "Mr. Reagan, and his Attorney General, Mr. Meese, have decided that they are going to turn back the clock on us. The purpose of movies like this is to make it acceptable to you."

The controversy was annoying to members of the film's company, especially to Oprah, who was interviewed, along with Margaret Avery and Akosua Busia, by *Los Angeles Times* reporter Jack Mathews about the movie.

What had struck her when she read the book was the element of sexual abuse in the story. Having had firsthand experience along those lines, she mentioned sexual abuse.

"That's what we should be talking about. If this film is going to raise some issues, I'm tired of hearing about what it's doing to the black men. Let's talk about the issues of wife abuse, violence against women, sexual abuse of children in the home.

"What the book did for me, and what the movie is doing

for other women who are sexually abused, is pointing up that you're not the only one."

All three actresses pointed out that they thought the protests against the movie were coming from "a small segment of racial watchdogs who are missing the movie's positive points."

"Every time there is a play or movie with white people in it," Oprah noted, "they don't expect them to represent the history of culture of the race. We aren't trying to depict the history of black people. It's one woman's story, that's all."

In an answering "letter to the editor," Legrand H. Clegg II, chairman of the Coalition Against Black Exploitation in Compton, California, took exception to Oprah's statement that no play or movie represents the history of culture.

"Blacks have continuously been stereotyped in movies since *Birth of a Nation,* and neither *The Color Purple, King Solomon's Mines,* or any other updated degradation of black people—which happens to also employ hungry black actors and actresses—is going to magically reverse this trend."

Singling out Oprah Winfrey's role of Sofia as one that would best illustrate "the potential damage of the movie," he continued: "In one scene, Sofia presents herself to the audience as a remorseless, unmarried, pregnant girl. Viewed alone this may seem harmless. But when coupled with the recollection of Bill Moyers's documentary on the 'Vanishing Black Family,' the weekly depicting of *Dynasty*'s Diahann Carroll as an illegitimate daughter/mother and the fact that 60 percent of all black children in America are born to unwed mothers, this scene, appearing in a movie rated PG-13, may well be a catastrophic image for black youths."

In the New York *Daily News,* columnist Earl Caldwell said: "*The Color Purple* can make you see red. That's especially true if you are a man and you happen to be black.

There is not much in the movie you want to see."

Frances Beal, in *Frontline*, a California newspaper, wrote: "A film which depicts the brutalization of a black woman by all the men in her life . . . can easily end up supporting the view that backward social relations within the family are the main problem with black America."

"It is a very dangerous film," wrote Leroy Clark, a professor of law at Catholic University. "The men are raping, committing incest, speaking harshly, separating people from their families, or they are incompetent, they can't fix a house or cook a simple meal. This is a lie to history. . . . It reinforces the notion of black men as beasts."

Roscoe Nix, president of the Montgomery County, Alabama, NAACP, said, "There was not a healthy black male in the movie."

Tony Brown, a television producer and columnist, put it this way: "I offer no excuses for the kinds of men that Walker wrote about. They are, for whatever reason, sad examples. But many of us who are male and black are too healthy to pay to be abused by a white man's movie focusing on our failures. And because so few films are produced with black themes, it becomes the only statement of black men."

Oprah Winfrey disagreed emphatically. "I was *surprised* to see the way people reacted to *The Color Purple*. I believe people see what they want to see in a work of art. When you see joy and beauty in something, it's because it's a part of you. When you see negative, anger and fear in something, it's because it is a part of you.

"I tell people that the movie was not for or against men. It's egotistical and macho for men to even think it's about them. *The Color Purple* is a novel about women."

With all the controversy, however, the movie did very well in its first seven weeks, grossing $39.2 million. It was also hailed by many critics—both black and white—as one of the ten best films of the year.

And then came the coup de grâce.

In February, when the Academy Awards were announced for films produced in 1985, *The Color Purple* was one of the most celebrated of the films mentioned, with eleven citations in all.

It was nominated for best picture, Whoopi Goldberg was nominated for best actress, and Margaret Avery and Oprah Winfrey were nominated for best supporting actress.

This was no small honor to Oprah! For her first movie role, to be nominated for an Oscar?—unbelievable!

Interestingly enough, when her father heard about that, he went to see the movie. It was the first picture he had seen in twenty-five years.

"I think I'd put Whoopi Goldberg first, Margaret Avery second, and maybe Oprah third," he said with a straight face. But then, Oprah knew, he was always a very tough taskmaster.

There was more, though. He went on: "Oprah has gone further than I ever thought of her going. She's come a long way. See, I can look back and see from where she came and I am proud that she made it. That was the beauty of *The Color Purple* movie for me: When the people were in the juke joint and the people over in the church were singing and the Lord ruled over the Devil, as I analyze it, and all the folks came out of the juke joint into the church. That was the part of it that practically made tears come into my eyes."

By the time she went to the Academy Awards, hopeful that she might indeed win, Oprah was almost a basket case. The problem was primarily her dress. She had paid a bundle to a designer who was doing it exclusively for her.

At the Beverly Wilshire Hotel the day before the Oscar

show, Oprah tried on the gown. The designer looked at her and said he wanted to taper it a little at the knee, and hem it. Oprah listened and agreed.

The next morning he brought the dress back. Oprah didn't try it on right away. About five minutes before she had to leave for the Dorothy Chandler Pavilion in downtown Los Angeles, she started to get into it.

"It would not go over my head or feet!" she said later. "Four people had to lay me on the floor and pull this gown on me! *On the floor*. Then they stood me up. The designer says, 'Do you have a girdle?' "

Oprah shouted right back: "No, I do not have a girdle! No!"

"I traveled to the Oscars on my back," Oprah related. "I was in the back of the limousine lying down. How to get out? How? I asked the driver to please stop a block before and I *rolled* out. Isn't that unbelievable? I sat in the gown all night and I couldn't breathe. I was afraid the seams were going to bust. If I leaned forward I cut off my windpipe and I could just pass out!"

And that was the way she spent the whole night.

"Not to mention that there were six standing ovations, and every time we stood up, I had to be pulled out of the chair. *Pulled out of the chair!* So I half lay in the chair all night, rigid. The one moment I didn't was when they read the nominees and the camera was on me. It was the worst."

Oprah felt that it was the lowest moment in her life.

"My best girlfriend was with me and she kept saying, 'How much is this gown costing you?' And I said, 'It has been drastically, *drastically* reduced. You can get this gown *real* cheap.' "

And then came the news. Oprah had not won.

In fact, the entire slate of the picture was almost totally ignored.

"I could not go through the night pretending that it was

okay that *Color Purple* did not win an Oscar. I was pissed and I was stunned. It was the worst night of my life."

But it wasn't over even then.

When she got back to the hotel:

"I was in a gown that had to be *cut off me*. Can you believe it?"

10
Going National

In the typically mindless way that things happen in the entertainment business, Oprah Winfrey was scheduled to shoot her scenes for her *second* motion picture the day after she was up for an Oscar and lost out for her *first* role.

The new picture was a film version of Richard Wright's classic novel *Native Son.* For the movie, Oprah had been cast as the mother of the hero, Bigger Thomas. She was a newcomer among a group of well-known actors and actresses—not the amateurs of *The Color Purple.* Nota bene: Geraldine Page. Elizabeth McGovern. Matt Dillon.

The story, of course, is set in the Chicago of the 1940s. Bigger Thomas, the hero, is a tortured young black man whose rage and frustration in the face of the virulent racism all about him drives him to express himself in the only way he feels he can—by the murder of a rich young white girl.

As Bigger's mother, Oprah played what she called "a very worn and tired thirty-six-year-old woman. It's a part where I had to be burdened, troubled, and weak—and I wanted to *be* that person."

Yet it was difficult work for Oprah. And, because of the irony of the Oscar loss: "It was the letdown, post-depression, or something." She tried to explain it. "It was the end of a chapter, the end of camp, the end of saying good-bye to all your friends, all the excitement. Then you wake up the next day, and it's over. Really over." It was time to pack up and go home.

But because it immediately followed the Oscar debacle, "It was good, because the character I played was a weary woman—tired, honey. It was good to have that, so I didn't have to *stretch* to play the character." Nevertheless, "It was exhausting. I really researched the role, but I was so glad to get it over with."

In an interview later she warned Regis Philbin and his viewers: "It's a very small role. Do not park your car if you intend to see me in this movie."

Roxanne T. Mueller, who interviewed Oprah in Cleveland, wrote: "She doesn't sound enthusiastic about her second acting effort, but it may be fatigue."

Apparently it was not fatigue. The motion picture opened to less than deafening accolades in December 1986. It was pulled shortly after opening.

This one failure did not put a total damper on Oprah's movie career. She was still anxious to continue.

She wanted to do a "lusty romantic role." And she had one in mind. "It's based on a true story Gloria Steinem told me about a prostitute who starts reading law books in jail and goes on to become a lawyer. So I'll get to be a hooker and have a pimp. Can't wait for that!"

If that did not work out, Oprah had another idea. "There aren't a lot of great roles for black women, so I'm going to start my own production company, and I'm also thinking about putting together a one-woman show."

She did indeed start her own production company, calling it Harpo Productions—"Harpo," of course, being "Oprah" spelled backward, and having nothing to do with the Marx Brothers or the character "Harpo" in *The Color Purple*!

"The scripts they send me are so mindless," she complained. "You wonder, 'Where in hell do they get these?' You would have to be a fool to do them—or desperate. That's one of the luxuries I have. I don't have to do movies to make money. I can do exactly what I feel like doing."

But that is getting a little ahead of the story.

When Oprah returned to Chicago from shooting *Native Son* in April 1986, she had become what is usually considered a "household word" in America. Once back on the job, she found that she was pulling even more viewers than she had previously attracted.

If there were any people in the entire Chicago area who had not heard of her, they were now quite aware of Oprah and of her particular place in the entertainment-world firmament.

During the summer of 1986 it was evident that Oprah Winfrey's share of the Oprah-Donahue audience had settled at about two to one. That is, for every Donahue viewer, there were two Oprah viewers.

"Fearless," "sassy," "unpredictable" were only a handful of the words used to describe her. Mainly, she was just a lot of fun to watch. Her show had become more and more Oprah-like over the months—and its 1986 version was becoming solid, sure-fire, and respectable.

Well—

"Respectable" was a word that might not always be used by *everyone* about the Oprah Winfrey morning offering. There were some appearances that might be termed embarrassing. There was the show in which the nudists appeared, and there was the man in drag who sang "Hit Me with Your Best Shot," and there was the "Husband of the Year Contest" held by Oprah to determine the best of the species. And there were her constant shows about weight loss and the "fats."

"Such spectacles can give the show a Marx Brothers quality that seems only sporadically intentional," wrote R. C. Smith in *TV Guide* in an otherwise laudatory article about the Oprah phenomenon.

She could do serious shows as well as these flaky ones. One elderly black man was reduced to weeping on her show as he described a lynching in the Deep South to which he had been a witness. Another woman burst into tears as she described the years of incest forced on her by her father.

(It was, incidentally, on that very show that Oprah Winfrey revealed that she as a child had been the victim of sexual abuse by her cousin and by her uncle—and by others as well.)

And there was the shocking story of the woman who told how she had felt when she was forced to shoot her abusive husband dead.

Oprah could be up and she could be down. But no matter where she was, she had full control of the show on which she appeared. She never let the reins slip out of her hands.

Talking about the program on which she revealed her own history of abuse as a child, Oprah said:

"It was something—the phones lit up with calls from women all over the country, saying the same thing had happened to them as girls. The guest I was interviewing started crying, and I started crying and told for the first time publicly that it had happened to me too."

As she gained firmer control of the direction of her show—and of herself—Oprah came to realize what it was that made her show a very special thing.

"I don't really have a big-name-guest kind of talk show. I'm more interested in people who have overcome some personal tragedy, or who have something to offer in terms of spiritual or emotional development. People out there think that I'm their girlfriend; they treat me like that. It's really *amaaazing*. I think that happens because I feel like I am. I feel that there's a common bond we all share."

What made her show different was its interest in "issues" more than "personalities."

"Rather than putting on a diet expert, we get a panel of people struggling to lose weight. Rather than interviewing a psychiatrist, we get people who've contemplated suicide to talk about depression."

As she continued interviewing people and talking to people in the audiences and on the telephone, she realized that there was little in the world that could shock her now. "I find what people say on television unusual, but it doesn't surprise me anymore. People have a *need* to tell someone, and the need overwhelms practicality."

One of her own secrets was the fact that she knew she was not exactly like everyone else.

"I take issue with people in this business who pretend they are like everybody else," she has said. "I certainly know what it's like not to be able to pay the mortgage, but I don't pretend now that I can't afford leather boots. I don't like pretending. I've said, when we have fashion shows, that I have spent eight hundred dollars on a dress, and it causes a lot of resentment."

Nevertheless, "The more I am able to be myself, the more honest and open I am, the more honest and open my guests and audience tend to be."

If she sensed resentment in people for the fact that she had money, she told them outright: "I'm thankful to you all for helping me to become what I am—which is a rich woman."

Other people in the talk-show business, she felt, kept a tighter rein on themselves, and did not allow themselves to talk about their wealth in front of other people. "You never know what they can or can't afford because they never tell you."

Even as she became more and more popular, she was

still the object of detractors. Not all the people in the print media were fans of hers or were even comfortable with her. P. J. Bednarski, the media business reporter for the *Chicago Sun-Times,* was less than enthralled with her manners on television.

He wrote that she ignored the moral and social issues involved in life, and talked quite amorally about orgasms, male sexual endurance, sex-organ size, and stars' "prowess" offscreen. He pointed out that quite frequently she lost control of the conversation and was unable to restrain her guests properly.

At one point, he wrote, a guest uttered "an unprintable slang expression for male ejaculation." That was proof to him that Oprah had some "growing up to do" as a talk-show hostess. He was also upset over some of her offhand questions that were offensive, such as the one when she had asked the porn actress if she ever got "sore."

"I think she's extremely entertaining, facile," he later admitted. "She has a way of being so natural on the air. Occasionally, that gets beyond her. It's pure honesty, I think. She just has to watch what she's doing."

Oprah's producer immediately riposted that no one but the critic in question had ever mentioned those two shows—the porn show and the sex-organ-size show—as being "tasteless." There were, in fact, no telephone calls to the station while they were on the air.

Besides, the "sexual size" show was one of the first to air after *A.M. Chicago* expanded to an hour-long program.

Oprah herself dismissed the controversy over the two shows Bednarski had zeroed in on.

"The porn show wasn't *about* the social issues. We do the shows people want to see, and I usually follow the mood of the audience. I was curious, they were curious. I asked every little thing we wanted to know.

"If I had to do it over again, I would not have been as loose as I was. I learned you should always do the honest thing, tell the audience you're as stumped as they are, go to a commercial if you're speechless."

At the end of each show there was always an outpouring of affection from the members of the audience. And Oprah took all this in in a gracious, friendly, and spontaneous manner. She greeted them all, hugging those she felt needed a hug, kissing others, posing for pictures from cameras gripped tightly in audience members' hands, signing autographs.

"You are more beautiful in person," some guests would say.

"You're just wonderful—please don't leave Chicago."

Each show was becoming more and more an outpouring of love and affection. And that was opiate to Oprah—who had once said something about love and hate that stuck in most people's minds:

"I have a fear of being disliked, even by people I dislike."

It was never "dislike" or "fear" or "opposition" that Oprah felt for Phil Donahue. If anything, what she felt for him was gratitude that he had brought the talk-show format to its present state of the art. Most of the "war" between Donahue and Oprah was manufactured outside Oprah and her show—and outside Donahue and his show.

"The media seem to want to create a war with Donahue," said Anne McGee, the publicist hired to generate media interest in Oprah at the time. "Oprah's answer has always been that he made her show possible by showing that women were interested in more than just mascara and beauty hints."

There had always been a difference, McGee said. "*Donahue* is admittedly a bit more cerebral than our show. We're a little more heartfelt."

Oprah's "image" by then was pretty accurately set in the public mind. Bill Zehme profiled her for *Spy* in this manner: "On her television program, Oprah Winfrey will hammer her thighs with knotty fists, cursing her corpulence. She will grandly toss her lacquered heap of hair and boulder through her audience, casting off gratuitous references to being spurned by men who left her 'swollen cow-faced' "—one of her patented "down-home" locutions—"from sobbing. Tugging at her trademark big-mama earrings, she will name-drop unashamedly—the most frequent is 'Steven' (her director in *The Color Purple,* Steven Spielberg)—and brashly interrogate guests who have come to parade their afflictions before the cameras.

"Capaciously built, black, and extremely noisy, Oprah Winfrey is an aberration among talk show doyennes, and her press materials bleat as much. She is awash in adjectival suds: *earthy, spontaneous, genuine, brassy, down-home.* 'The adorable token dumpling' is how one public relations executive describes her. A hyperkinetic amalgam of Mae West, Reverend Ike, Richard Simmons, and Hulk Hogan is more to the point."

That was Oprah, right down to the smallest detail. All that was lacking in the description at the time was the fact that exactly like other celebrities who had come into the big time, Oprah had picked up her own entourage of gofers, sycophants, and just plain admirers. Or the fact that she loved to make telephone calls from the backseats of stretch limousines. Or the fact that she wore a full-length fox fur, dyed purple, to a New York premiere.

With the money rolling in, she was making other important adjustments in her life-style. Most conspicuously, in the summer of 1986 she purchased for almost $1 million—$850,000 was the recorded figure—a high-rise condominium situated on the lakefront in one of Chicago's poshest residential sections.

It was a magnificent suite—fifty stories up—with a number of real "wow" features: marble floors, four bathrooms, a sauna, and a wraparound view of Lake Michigan. It had a wine cellar, too, and a crystal chandelier that lit up *inside* her closet when she opened the door! In one of the bathrooms there was even a marble tub, with gold dolphins for spigots.

The place had been owned previously by Evangeline Gouletas, the millionairess tycoon who left it when she married Hugh Carey, the one-time governor of New York State.

"Of course," Oprah told a friend, "there's not a stick of furniture in the place now, because *my* decorator threw all my old stuff out."

Even without an overload of furniture, Oprah would come home, kick off her downtown clothes, fill that marble tub with a whole bottle of bubble bath, and soak a good long time, staring in disbelief at the gold dolphins in front of her.

Then she would put on her flowered pajamas and a pair of fat socks, make herself some popcorn in the brand-new microwave, and stare out at that wraparound view of Lake Michigan.

"Girl!" she would tell herself. "Look at you! You're not on the farm in Mississippi feeding those chickens no more!"

Indeed she was not.

"It is so great living up here. The sun rises off the lake in the morning, right through this window—and it's a joy to my soul! Good Lord, I do feel blessed!"

One of her close associates viewed it with some astonishment after she had purchased it and moved in. "This place is strictly a Greek palace," was the comment.

But great for New Year's Eve parties. At the turn of the year, Oprah entertained *Ebony-Jet* heiress publisher Linda Johnson Rice—*and* the Reverend Jesse Jackson.

Top that!

When she was not engaged in entertaining, she was being invited out herself. She visited Abra Prentice Wilkin, a Rockefeller heiress, at her home in Chicago. Wilkin reported that Oprah "was like a little kid running around my apartment, just oohing and aahing."

Sugar Rautbord, a socialite and successful novelist, invited her over to her place for a visit. Rautbord reported that Oprah moved quickly about the apartment, looking at this and that.

"Oooh, where'd you get this? Oooh, how much did you pay for that?"

"There's a wonderful hunger about her," Rautbord said. "Some people yearn to be free. Oprah yearns to be rich."

Oprah's success was tied directly to the success of *A.M. Chicago,* the show that had launched her. And as Oprah's image increased in clout and intensity in astronomic proportions, so did the size and majesty of the show.

In August 1984, the show, as reported, had been expanded to an hour. As it continued to attract more viewers, it was finally deemed to be not just a talk show about and for Chicagoans, but a talk show that had no limitations other than those of its star.

Thus, in September 1985, the brass at WLS-TV decided that Oprah had made it into something very special in her own image. The show's title was changed from *A.M. Chicago* to *The Oprah Winfrey Show*. There was a very good reason for this.

While Oprah was up front with her show and her new personality and her new life-style, a lot of very important things were going on in the deep background. As early as 1985, a national syndicator had become interested in the show as a property—and in Oprah as a client.

One of the most successful syndication operations in the country, King World had built the game show *Wheel of Fortune* into a huge money-maker for Merv Griffin, who owned it.

And so it was that Stuart Hersch, chief operating officer of King World Productions Inc., began talks with Oprah and WLS-TV early on about syndicating the show. Of course, its name would have to be changed to *The Oprah Winfrey Show* for syndication to succeed—and that's why it was changed.

A satisfactory deal was worked out, with Oprah's representative, attorney-manager Jeffrey Jacobs, to market the show as a syndicated effort. Syndicating the show meant selling it over the counter to independent stations, as explained in Chapter 1. By October 1985 the show was on the block for any station—independent or network—to purchase. The target date for syndication was set for September 1986.

From a practical standpoint, it would take at least a year to determine how the show would do financially, especially against the formidable competition of Phil Donahue. And so a concerted effort was mounted to "sell" Oprah Winfrey on a national scale all during the twelve months between October 1985 and September 1986.

Oprah cooperated hugely—first by becoming a big hit in *The Color Purple,* second by being nominated for an Academy Award, and third by continuing to draw viewers to her local Chicago show.

As part of the push, *Variety* took a look at the show. Along with the information at the end of the review that the show was going into national syndication in September 1986, the piece would alert scores of independent station owners to the existence and potential of the show. That was the way things were done in the business.

In *Variety*'s TV review section, "Mor." wrote that "Many of the terms best used to describe Winfrey and the show —candor, vulnerability, accessibility—are in short supply on TV and, judging from the response, not too plentiful in real life."

Pointing out that since Oprah's arrival on the show in January 1984 (when it was still a half-hour format and without "Oprah Winfrey" in the title), "the ratings started going up and they never stopped until she had taken as much of a share of her time period as any show could possibly take."

He also wrote, "The immediacy of her success is a reflection of the immediacy of her show, of every show she does. The feeling is that when the red light goes on, you get all of Oprah. She has taken the potential of intimacy of television to its outermost limits, or at least where the limit is now. It is an intimacy that to date has been heard largely on radio and really has never been explored fully on TV."

In the review when it was noted that the show was going national, it added that 118 markets had already signed up.

"Much has been made of her kicking the ratings pins out of 'Donahue' in Chicago and that she will be facing him in many markets in syndication. It will be a tight race wherever they go head-to-head, with the probable edge going to Winfrey. She's new, fresh, and different and has a sense of the medium that comes around only about once a decade."

Oprah made a number of promotional tapes, showing herself and scenes from her best shows. In addition, she took on a heavy promotional tour during the late summer, holding press conferences in many of the major cities in America, all as a way to plug her syndication.

She was good at it. She had done the other side herself, interviewing people on just that same kind of promotional tour. She understood what to do. And she made it look very good. The stories written about her introduced her to millions of people who had never heard of her before—people in San Francisco, in San Diego, in Kansas City, in almost any city where she had never been.

Strategically, the year-long marketing campaign for *The Oprah Winfrey Show* was a classic:

The first step was for King World to gauge how Oprah Winfrey would affect viewers in the parts of the country that had never seen her. To do this, tapes of Oprah's shows were sent to "focus groups"—to use the jargon of the broadcasting trade—in specific locales for a look-see.

The question was: Could an overweight, earthy black woman succeed in places where women on television were usually thin, blond, and soft-spoken? Would Oprah's sass and unpredictability kill her off before she could get away from the starting line?

The answers from these test groups proved to be overwhelmingly positive *for* Oprah.

The next step was to show these tapes to television groups—small network-type alliances of a half-dozen or more stations owned and operated by one head. These group responses proved positive too—so much so that each group wanted exclusive broadcast rights for all their stations.

Because this would mean precluding the possibility of selling the show to an individual station at a possibly higher price, King World withdrew these blanket offers and took a big gamble: It decided to open negotiations separately in each city and market area. Oprah's track record proved that she was a hot enough commodity to win better deals through separate negotiations with individual stations.

The following step was to mount a big ad campaign in the television media publications telling the story of Oprah's thrashing of Donahue not only in Chicago but also earlier in Baltimore. As the blitz of the ad campaign continued, King World would dicker with individual stations—leaking sudden information about a big new market that "had just signed up"—and all that kind of thing.

During this phase, the "Donahue-buster" strategy was dropped for a milder approach that would not tend to make Oprah look arrogant or conceited. The idea was to stress her talent and her personality. And the media generally ate this up.

Always hungry for new faces and images, they took to her ecstatically. She was now on a real roll—even after that unfortunate loss at the Academy Awards. In fact, her loss may even have built up some sympathy for her among the in-types who knew show business for what it was.

On the eve of the Donahue confrontation—when Oprah was going to go national—she had signed up with 180-odd stations. That was a bit less than "King" Donahue's 200-plus, but within easy range. Now the outcome was all in the laps of the gods.

Oprah and Donahue did meet head-on, September 8, 1986, as was narrated in detail earlier. The *big* question was not yet settled. Oprah won the battle. But the *war* would stretch on into the future.

How many of the signed-up stations would stick with her?

How many stations would renew for the full year?

How many would cancel out and drop her?

Three months would tell the story.

Oprah was exhausted. She needed a little recharging of her personal batteries after that wild spring and summer of spieling and selling. She needed what combat troops need—a little R and R. A little Rest and Recreation.

It was an interesting call for Oprah. What she did was telephone her father in Nashville and tell him she was coming down to spend Thanksgiving with the family.

It was a good rest for her. Once in Nashville, she slumped down to relax and renewed her acquaintance with her father and stepmother.

And there was an important side trip—to Kosciusko! A little bit of checking out of her roots.

"We went to Mississippi together," her father reported. "She went by the old church where she gave her first speech, and she visited all the old folk. She was so candid!"

Oprah *loved* visiting Kosciusko. It brought back memories, and sometimes just the trace of a tear in her eye. Her father was always standing there, proudly beaming at her.

"She saw this one elderly lady sitting on her porch," he

said, "and Oprah wanted to know if she wanted her to bring in any firewood."

Vernon Winfrey shook his head with a smile.

"She's still level-headed. Her feet are on the ground."

That satisfied him and made him feel that he had indeed brought her up right.

After that lovely interval in the Deep South, Oprah returned to the gold dolphins on her marble bathtub and flexed her muscles to get back into the swing of things.

Show after show.

Three months later, when quiet had once again settled over the talk-show battleground, the incredible results finally were in—and King World and Oprah were rubbing their hands in glee and astonishment.

Witness:

On its front page on December 31, 1986, *Variety* headlined Oprah's success:

WINFREY'S WHAMMO SYNDIE DEAL

with the subhead reading:

SHOW GROSSES $125-MIL, SHE GETS $30,000,000

The story said that *The Oprah Winfrey Show* was almost sure to gross $125 million for the 1987–88 season, and up to $150 million for the following 1988–89 season.

The deal itself was wilder than anybody had thought it might be. Oprah herself would get one quarter of the gross "right off the top." She would be in a position to pocket more than $31 million in 1987–88, making her the highest-paid performer in show business.

In addition to that, she had signed a five-year contract with King World to host the series through the 1990–91 season.

Meanwhile, Oprah herself was doing all she could outside the confines of her show to build up her image and increase her clout. At least four nights a week, she went out on speaking engagements. Most of these were done gratis—at churches, at Y's, at shelters for the homeless or for teenage runaways. Sometimes she would be out with what she called "little sisters"—a group she and some friends formed in 1985 with eleven-year-olds from the Cabrini-Green housing project in Chicago.

Typically, to this group she might say something along these lines:

"I know how easy it is to think you know everything. But life is a constant growth process. If you think you know it all now, you're kidding yourself."

She might then point out that it was impossible to make it without the proper education. "Education is essential to preparing yourself for the right opportunity," she might say. "You really do have to believe that somewhere there is a way out."

Nothing would keep her from making some off-the-cuff comment in the middle of *any* talk:

"I'm a born ham! You give me three people—and I'm *on*! Having an audience makes for a better day."

Not all her speaking engagements were in Chicago or even Illinois. When she was not in the environs of the city, she might be in another state, or in another area of the country.

Out of the blue came a call from the *60 Minutes* television show. The word was that "himself"—Mike Wallace—was coming to do an interview with Oprah. It had been set up earlier, but had been postponed for one reason or another.

Oprah was floored. "Mike Wallace!" she cried. "Lordy be! Is there something the matter with my taxes?"

If there was anyone in America—or the universe—who had not yet heard of Oprah Winfrey by now, he or she would no longer be in the dark after Mike Wallace was through with her.

The show aired on December 14, 1986. Wallace introduced her as the hostess of a "colorful and controversial" talk show in Chicago. Wallace then said she had gone national in syndication three months before that and her audience rating had "soared."

He quoted her: "I was like a hit album waiting to be released. I knew my day would come."

Oprah came on, and explained her gift of being herself on camera, which lets her say, "Hey, there, how are you doing?" to people she cannot even see.

Wallace gave a brief thumbnail sketch of her early life, bringing her up to Baltimore.

> OPRAH: [Baltimore] was sixty pounds ago.
> WALLACE (amused): You were sixty pounds lighter?
> OPRAH: Sixty pounds ago. I think of my life in terms of my thighs.

She told about the French perm and how she felt being a "bald black anchorwoman," and how she was demoted to a small talk show, and how she had started to "wing it"—and how it was like "breathing" to her.

Then Chicago and—success!

"The reason I communicate with all these people," she told him, "is because I think I'm every woman and I've had every malady and I've been on every diet, and I've had—oh, men who have done me wrong, honey. So I *related* to all of that. And I'm not afraid or ashamed to say it. So whatever is happening, if I can relate to it personally, I always do."

Wallace asked her if she felt that she got the "truth" from the people she talked to. She said she thought she did. Wallace then told the viewers: "Although she talks about all kinds of things, one of her favorite subjects is something she feels is missing in her own life: how to catch and keep a man."

A clip from one of Oprah's shows followed, showing Oprah in conversation with one of her guests.

OPRAH: You're in the grocery store line, he's ahead of you, he's getting ready to leave. What do you say in that short amount of time so that you can establish some contact later on?

GUEST: Okay. I'd say, "You're very attractive. I'd like to spend some time with you."

OPRAH (screams): I can't say *that*!

Wallace then spoke to Oprah: "I would think you could be a pretty tough lady for a fellow to handle. Come on. Ambitious. Out front. You really don't have much time, honestly, for a guy. You've got time for yourself for now."

"I think that I'd be really great with some guy," she admitted, "but I'm not going to go around hoping and praying for it anymore. If it happens it happens. If it doesn't, I'll get a kitten."

"Television every day is where you'll get to know Oprah," Wallace told the camera, "and she's confident you'll get to like her."

And Oprah was confident things would work out just fine.

"It's going to do well. If it doesn't, I will still do well. I will do well because I am not defined by a show. You know, I think we are defined by the way we treat ourselves and the way we treat other people. It would be wonderful to be acclaimed as, you know, 'Talk-Show Host Who's Made It.' That would be wonderful. But if that doesn't happen, there are other important things in my life."

WALLACE: And a fellow?

OPRAH (no answer; she just hums)

WALLACE: That's the one thing you're not sure of.

OPRAH (continues humming): No, I think it will happen. It'll happen. I keep saying it. But now I say to myself, I lose forty pounds, maybe it'll happen then. Maybe it'll happen. You know, before the movie, I said, It'll happen after the movie. Then before the Oscars, It'll happen. I don't know. I think it will. If it doesn't, I may come a-calling on you.

And *that* was another typical Oprah-ism!

11
The Wit and Wisdom of Oprah Winfrey

From the beginning it was obvious that Oprah Winfrey possessed something quite out of the ordinary in the way of personality, outlook, and overall persona. When she spoke, people listened—to paraphrase another paraphrase. When the Ku Klux Klan wives turned down her invitation to lunch, she responded with an unbelieving comment: "Even if I *paid* for it?"

In time her remarks came to be known as "Oprah-isms."

Oprah-isms cover all subjects imaginable. Maxisubjects, minisubjects, subsubjects, and so on. She talks a lot about men and sex and food and fat and money and success and the business of getting along with your life.

"Doing talk shows is like breathing to me," she has said. "It's been a living hoot!"

Another Oprah-ism.

Many Oprah-isms fit into no definite category at all. Others do. So as not to belabor the point, there is not only wit in the best of the Oprah-isms, but wisdom as well.

Hence the chapter title "The Wit and Wisdom of Oprah Winfrey."

They fall broadly into certain subject areas—but many of them fit into no known category at all. But—so what? Here they are!

Referring to the now well-known remark made by a guest who had not had an orgasm in eighteen years of marriage until she put herself in the hands of a sexual surrogate, Oprah said:

"You know, there's walking up to the line. I've danced on the line, but *this*! *This* was absolutely *over* the line!"

About all the publicity hype expended in building her up into a "national" figure to promote the syndication of her show, Oprah remarked:

"I'm beginning to feel marketed, you know? I'm beginning to feel like I'm 'packaged realism.' Which doesn't make me feel too comfortable, because I just am what I am. I'll be glad once the show has started [its national run] and people can judge for themselves. The hype is more than I can handle. I feel like I have to be the Second Coming. And I'm not. I'm just Oprah. Plain old Oprah."

In a promotional piece for an upcoming show on self-made millionaires, Oprah confessed that her love life was sagging and needed a bit of bolstering up—preferably by somebody like a self-made millionaire:

"If there is a six-foot-two-inch black man who fits this category, please, please *come in*!"

There have been many remarks made by Oprah Winfrey about the "Mr. Right" she has been looking for all her life. Here are a few of them:

Asked once if she was "concerned" about "getting married," she responded with candor:

"No, I haven't given up. But I've stopped worrying about it. I think that if you're an intelligent, successful black woman in the eighties, you're going to have a difficult time finding a mate who is supportive. Mr. Right either will or will not happen for me, and I'm not going to stand still waiting for him."

"[Mr. Right would be] taller than me, smarter than me, and not threatened by me. He would have to be outgoing but know when to shut up. And I don't think it would matter if he was black, white, or Chinese."

More specs about "Mr. Right":

"That he be tall, that he have his own money, and that he be spiritually grounded. Everything that happens to you happens for a reason—everything you do in your life comes back to you. I call it 'Divine Reciprocity.' That's why I try to be kind to people—more for my sake than theirs."

"It's very important for me to have a man I can look up to. I like them tall and I like them smart. [That combination] is not an easy thing to find, but it will happen."

"Lots of people want to ride with you in the limo. But you want someone who'll be there when the limo breaks down, who'll help you catch the bus."

And the capper:

"Mr. Right's coming, but he's in Africa, and he's *walking*!"

Oprah occasionally worries about her love life when total absence of a male counterpart is the status quo:

"I don't even have a goldfish. I would love to have a *significant other* in my life. That would be wonderful. But everything in life is about timing, and obviously the timing is not right for me now."

Thoughts on "dating," and "sex," and "men" in general:

"I don't need the kind of 'dating' when you're going out with a man just to go out. If it's not going to be a meaningful relationship—and I can tell you in three minutes if it is or not—then I don't waste my time. So I go through periods where I don't see anyone. Like now. It's not intentional, just sort of a de facto celibacy."

About that all-important "timing" in the proper male-female relationship:

"Actually, I believe you *can* have it all, but I also believe that nothing happens before its time. And maybe I'm just not ready to have a man in my life right now. But it's the saddest thing. I'll tell you, that's been the price. That has definitely been the price."

Of primary consideration to Oprah is the problem of weight. She has been up and she has been down. But it seems always to be a problem, lurking off there in the distance somewhere, waiting to pounce on her. And, of course, it is every bit as important to her as the men in her life are. Here are some of her thoughts on weight.

She was once asked if she thought her weight had anything to do with her single status. She shot back immediately:

"If you don't have a man, you need spaghetti."

In a discussion about why she had spent some time at a health spa in Tucson, she commented:

"I'm lucky because I live in the public eye and people treat me positively. But there are also people who think they can one-up me. They say, 'She may have a talk show, she may have been nominated for an Oscar, but she's still got fat thighs!' "

On a show a guest once suggested that if she go in seriously for permanent weight loss, she might alter her own personality for the worse. Oprah sprang on her:

"Girl, I tell people all the time—my personality is *not* in my behind!"

She is always conscious about her weight and build:

"Women, always black—three hundred to four hundred pounds—waddle up to me, rolling down the street, and they say, 'You know, people are always confusing me for you.' I know when they're coming. I say, 'Here comes another woman who thinks she looks like me.' "

She has been many different sizes and shapes:

"I know, I know. I carry it well. But it's driving me nuts. I'm five-six. In Baltimore, I weighed one forty-eight. When I was Miss Tennessee, I weighed one thirty-five. You can see my bones at one thirty-five. But when I moved to Chicago, I started *really* putting on the pounds. I think I wanted that weight as a defense, so if the show failed, I could blame it on that. Same thing with me. As long as I'm heavy, I've got a great excuse. But I tell you, this is the biggest, biggest problem in my life. Not being able to have the self-discipline to beat this. It truly makes me real *depressed*."

Going on a heavy diet and sticking strictly to it doesn't always make her feel any better in the cold bright light of day:

"I was walking down the street yesterday and I see this little round butterball of a lady. She leans over the balcony and hollers at me, 'Let's hear it for fat women!' I guess I haven't come as far as I thought."

She once told Joan Rivers that she inherited her weight problem:

"I got my weight from my grandfather cows, my aunt cows, and my cousin cows."

Summing up the weight problem in general, Oprah says:

"I do have black woman's behind. It's a disease God inflicted upon the black women of America."

In spite of her weight, Oprah *loves* food. She *loves* to eat. It's her second most favorite fun in life:

"My idea of heaven is a great big baked potato—and someone to share it."

She eats when she feels depressed sometimes, to relieve the gloom, and she eats when she feels extremely happy, to celebrate:

"Sometimes when I can't decide whether I'm tired or hungry, I make the decision while I'm eating."

It's not easy to sit down to a meal of any kind if you feel the way Oprah does about her weight and her appearance:

"I hate people with great metabolisms. You don't know what it's like unless food controls your life. For everything I put into my mouth, I either feel like, 'Okay, I'm going to let myself do it,' or I feel guilt about it. There's not one thing that I eat that I don't think about or regret later."

In general:

"I really, *really* like food. It's my comfort, my warm hug."

The really horrible thing about going on a diet is that it simply doesn't work:

"I know I cannot deprive myself and be the same person. I have to figure out a way to do it. I've been on every diet: Stillman, Atkins, Beverly Hills, Fit for Life. I've done every one. I *gained* on the Scarsdale Diet!"

Except for keeping her weight down and failing at diets, Oprah's life is so upscale that she can hardly believe it. Success is the most pleasant surprise of her life—and yet she knew she would be a success all along.

How does it feel to be a success?

"It feels very good. Everything has its time and place. I look upon it as part of a process. I've been warming up for a long time. I've been in broadcasting since I was seventeen. I tell people, 'You are responsible for your own life.' I take full responsibility for my successes and failures, from getting up and getting my own talk show to losing my luggage on a trip."

Someone once asked Oprah if her film career conflicted with her talk-show career. She replied:

"Absolutely not. People can do anything they want to do in this life—and I intend to keep doing both."

But how about balancing a personal life at the same time you are balancing a double career?

"It's *impossible*. I learned that you can't change other people. Only yourself."

Is there any special secret to success?

"The whole path to success is not as difficult as some people would want you to believe. The process was the goal. I've taken great joy in the process. My main concern about myself now is whether I will live up to my potential; I already reach more people than many politicians ever do."

How does the future look to Oprah?

"When I look into the future, it's so bright *it burns my eyes*!"

Her type of popularity is quite different from that of other celebrities. She revels in this difference. For example:

"People don't stop me on the street like a star and flutter and ask for my autograph. They stop me and say, 'Wait right *here*! I'm going to get a pen,' or they see me coming down the block and say, '*Hey,* come here!' "

When asked whether the days she spent on a farm in her early isolated rural life might not have been the best ones of all, rather than these busy, stressful, tension-ridden days now, Oprah snorts:

"Who are we kidding? *These* are!"

Is life different, now that she is famous?

"I'll tell you. I understand that I'm no different than anyone else. And there's nothing that I will experience that other people haven't already felt."

Is her success a surprise to her?

"I always knew I was going to do well in life. I always believed that whatever I wanted for myself I could get."

What about the huge sums of money? Have they made a difference? How can Oprah keep her head with all that money around her?

> "I'm humored by people who think I can lose my head over this. I have such stable roots that I understand that all of this is relative. None of this *defines* who I am."

Oprah is today a grown-up version of what she was as a tiny child: "The Preacher." She continues to preach to anyone who will listen. For example, she preaches a lot to teenage girls, trying to warn them about early pregnancy and irresponsibility.

Here are two items from "Oprah's Law," part of a talk she gives to teenagers about pregnancy and education:

- "Get pregnant and I'll break your face! Don't tell me you want to do great things in your life and still not be able to tell a boy no. [If] you want something to love and to hug, tell me and I'll buy you a puppy."
- "If you cannot talk correctly, if you cannot read or do math, if you become pregnant, if you drop out of school, you will never have a Cadillac—I guarantee it! Don't tell me you want to do great things in your life if all you carry to school is a radio!"

She has always understood what the term "falling in love" really means:

> "My father always said, 'When you fall, you fall so *hard*.' And it seemed to be true. I'd fall for some guy and it would be life or death. But maybe I've been in love once—truly in love."

Sometimes Oprah varies the speech to teenage girls, and warns them about getting pregnant and having babies this way:

"If you want affection you don't need a baby. Get a kitten!"

Oprah doesn't always have the best lines in her programs. Many times the Oprah-isms are reactions to what Oprah says, or answers to Oprah's questions.

On one show, Oprah had asked members of the audience to write down their sexual fantasies.

OPRAH [glancing down at the sheet of paper in her hand]: Is this one of your fantasies—to have your thighs kissed?

WOMAN (ecstatically): Yeah! All the way to the top!

On one show a member of the audience felt sorry for Richard Lewis, a professional comedian whose shtick was having trouble with dating women.

WOMAN: I wonder if you'd like to go out with my sister? She's not Jewish, but she whines a lot.

OPRAH: That's an ethnic slur!

LEWIS: It's hard for me to relate to that in response. Unless there's a picture and résumé—

WOMAN (indicating woman beside her): How about this girl right here?

LEWIS: She's lovely. But you know, I'm just getting over a breakup, so I need about three, four years to get over it.

On a show called "Overweight and Liking It," some overweight members in the audience really did *not* like it. A woman in the audience addressed one of the "fat and happy" guests.

WOMAN: How can you be happy sitting in the bathtub? As an overweight person, I know: You turn to wash yourself, and all the water is in front of the tub because you're fat, and you're lying all over the tub, and you have no water behind you to even wash yourself with!

OPRAH: Someone just called out: "Take a shower!"

Several professional comedians, including Wil Shriner, Herb Shriner's son, and Louie Anderson, were discussing the effect humor had on their early lives:

OPRAH: In high school were all the girls anxious to date you because you were so funny?

SHRINER: No, no. I wasn't funny in high school.

OPRAH: When did you get funny?

SHRINER: Everybody was funny in high school, weren't they? Seemed to me like everybody was funny in high school.

ANDERSON: I wasn't really funny in high school either.

OPRAH: No?

ANDERSON: No, I wasn't.

SHRINER: What amazed me was that everyone got jobs, you know.

Again, on the show "Overweight and Liking It," a male telephone caller began challenging Joan Belotta, one of the "happy fats" on the panel:

CALLER: I don't think I'd want to go to bed with someone who's going to overdominate me in the bedroom.

OPRAH: What do you mean, *overdominate?*

BELOTTA: It means you're on top and he's on the bottom.

OPRAH (moans): Joan! Oooh, Joan! We're going to break for a commercial after that!

A guest on a show about infidelity confessed to carrying on three simultaneous affairs with other men—and still finding time enough to take care of her husband. Oprah was curious about how she could manage that. The woman responded:

"It takes a lot of attention to detail."

One of Oprah's shows featured guests who suffered deformities of one kind or another. The idea was to discuss how they coped with these disabilities. To a woman with no hands, Oprah somewhat absently observed that she probably had difficulty putting on a dress with twenty buttons. The woman snapped back:

"Yeah. Probably not unlike *you* trying to get into pantyhose."

12
The Wit and Wisdom of Oprah Winfrey II

One of the subjects that is never far from the surface in Oprah Winfrey's life is the subject of black-white relations. Oprah's position has been stated many times, but there are still rampant misunderstandings about it.

For example, there are those who say that Oprah Winfrey on her show is playing the typical "Mammy" role—the "Aunt Jemima thing"—to suit the whites in the audience.

To this, Oprah has responded:

> "I hear this. I hear this a lot. I hear that I don't hug the black people the way I hug the white people, that I go to the white people in the audience first. First of all, there are *more* white people. There just are more! I could not survive with this show if I only catered to black people. I just could not! I couldn't be where I am if I did. That's not what it's about!"

To those who say she is too soft on whites, Oprah frequently counters with the following statement from a speech she made to an all-white group, tweaking their middle-class noses just a bit. The subject was "whipping"—the kind of discipline she got in her childhood:

> "Oh, so you women *do* know what a 'switch' is. I thought that all of you here had profound discussions with your three-year-olds: 'Oh, Jennifer, do you want to tell Mummy why you were bad?' "

But she isn't on the bandwagon when the demonstrators begin waving placards and shouting for civil rights:

> "Whenever I hear the words 'community organization,' or 'task force,' I know I'm in deep trouble. People feel you have to lead a civil rights movement every day of your life, that you have to be a spokeswoman and represent *the race*. I understand what they're talking about, but you don't have to do it, don't have to do what other people want you to do. Blackness is something I just am. I'm black. I'm a woman. I wear a size ten shoe. It's all the same to me."

And, of course, Chicago is the place to practice "race relations," it being split right down the middle:

> "Some people say, 'Oprah, you're not black enough. You don't do enough interviews with blacks, you hug more whites than blacks, you get more white people in the audience.' I tell them I look for the best possible guest, someone who can add to the conversation, someone who's articulate. No, I'm not saying black people aren't articulate, but I can't say, 'You can turn on the set every day and see black people on my show.' For us to transcend race, sexual bias, and hatred in Chicago, the most racist city in the country, is really something. I would get phone-ins from white people who would say, 'Oprah, we love you, we watch you every day, but don't come around our neighborhood.' "

About her blackness, Oprah frequently becomes quite vociferous:

"There are still a lot of black people who are very angry and bitter. They want me to be just as angry and bitter, and I won't be. It just burns me. . . . Some black people say I'm not black enough. I wonder, how black do you have to be?"

About color-consciousness:

"It doesn't matter to me what color people are. I try to see their souls first."

How she feels about being what she is and what she is doing for others like her:

"I am one black woman. The drums of Africa still beat in my heart. They will not let me rest until every black boy and every black girl has had a chance to prove their worth. One black woman."

Oprah Winfrey was assigned one mile of the four-thousand-mile chain of hand-holding Americans on May 25, 1986, in the Hands Across America demonstration to raise money for the poor:

"My mile will be for people who can't afford the ten-dollar [standing fee]. No rich people in *my* mile."

What Oprah's success in the Chicago area proves to her about her own position on race:

"Chicago is one of the most racially volatile cities anywhere. Our success there shows that race and sex can be transcended."

There is a lot of philosophy in Oprah Winfrey's statements about life, about attitudes, and about courage. Following are a few of them—some inspirational, some amusing, some simply instructive.

One truth that Oprah feels deeply:

"Every day the job is a challenge. It's simply important to me to be the best I can be. And in this business, if you're good, it speaks for itself."

And another:

"I think that the path of our spiritual involvement is the greatest journey we all take. And I think that is part of the reason why I am as successful as I have been, because success wasn't the goal. The process was. I wanted to do good work. I wanted to do well in my life."

Still another Oprah-ism:

"Luck is when preparation meets opportunity."

Oprah believes in "energizing" herself every morning before she goes to work. How does she do it?

"What I do every morning is I go to my window. I watch the sun come up and I center myself and try to touch the God light that I believe is in all of us. Some people call it prayer, some people call it meditation; I just call it 'centering up.' I get boundless, boundless energy from that. If there happens to be a day when I don't do it, I find myself loose, misdirected. I try to approach every show as if I hadn't done it ever before."

What is Oprah's outlook on her life and the way she is living it?

"I'm truly blessed. But I also believe that you tend to *create* your own blessings. You have to prepare yourself so that when opportunity comes, you're ready."

When she was four years old and living on her grandmother's farm down in Mississippi, Oprah used to hear their visitors talk about life's trials and tribulations. It was an important lesson to her:

"That was the moment I knew I was different. I listened and I didn't *believe* I was like that. And if you believe you weren't meant for that kind of life, you go out and *create* a better life."

Oprah insists that she is a *now* person—someone involved in life from one minute to the next. She's not really *saving* anything of herself for tomorrow:

"Wasting time bugs me, and it's a waste of time when people worry about tomorrow, or a year from now, or five years from now. If you just hit high C and hold the note, tomorrow *comes*."

Oprah often gives advice to people who ask her how she has been able to accomplish so much and become such an important personality in her time:

"Don't follow in *my* footsteps. Initiate your own guidance. Often intuition will direct you. If it feels right, it's probably right."

There is still a lot of that young preacher in Oprah Winfrey, even to this day:

"It's not so much a voice. A lot of people ask God for help and then wait for thunder and lightning. You have to be *receptive* enough to heed the call when it comes!"

Oprah has a lot of ideas about why she has been successful as an interviewer and hostess on television. Sometimes she says this:

"When people watch television, they are looking to see themselves. I think the reason why I work as well as I do on the air is that people *sense* the realness."

Communicating on television involves "building a bond with the viewer," through sharing doubts, emotions, problems, failures, and even fears. Oprah says:

"They connect to these same kinds of emotions. People love to see themselves reflected in you."

Getting kicked around, Oprah feels, makes her more receptive to the hang-ups of others:

"Thank goodness I was raised by my grandmother the first six years, then sent to live with my mother, and then with my father. Because of the various environments I was exposed to, I am better able to understand what others have gone through."

And there's always that key personality factor, Oprah's "vulnerability":

"I am exactly that same way out there as I am here talking to you. No different. You have to let yourself be vulnerable, let people see you as something other than a broadcaster. Doing this is as natural to me as breathing."

When a solemn middle-aged man on her show said that after surgery to correct impotence his testicles had inflated to the size of basketballs, Oprah reacted quickly:

"Wait a minute! How do you *walk* with testicles the size of basketballs?" (Although the obvious answer to *that* question would have been "With great difficulty," no answer at all was forthcoming.)

Oprah's toughest interview was the one she had with Barbara Walters:

"Why? Barbara Walters was my mentor, Barbara is my *idol*! It's hard to interview people you really, *really* like, because you're *gaga*. You go through a period where—it's a Yiddish expression, 'kvelling'—you start kvelling and you say, 'Oh, I love you, and I love you so much, and I love you all the time, and I love your dress, and I love your beads, and I love your hair.' " (At this point Barbara Walters interrupted her and added the obvious punchline: "—I just don't like *you*.")

As Oprah met South African Bishop Desmond Tutu at a party in Chicago, she hugged him, and he hugged her in return. And she said:

"Bishop Tutu wouldn't hug Phil Donahue!"

Another Oprah-ism relating to "himself":

"I'm a great mimic. I'll ride with a cab driver who speaks Spanish, and I'll start talking with a Spanish accent. That's why I make it a practice never to watch Phil Donahue. I'm afraid I'll begin to look like him."

A very special Sunday-type Oprah-ism:

"Last Sunday I was in church and a deacon tapped me on the knee and asked for my autograph. I told him, 'I don't do autographs in church. Jesus is the star here.' "

In a conversation with best-selling author Jackie Collins:

JACKIE: I think today women are looking for brains rather than brawn [in their heroes].

OPRAH: Yeah, but brawn's not bad. *Brawn's not bad.*

A housewife-prostitute, explaining the details of her profession, said she was working on an "agency" basis. They would page her on a beeper, she would go to work, and then return home. Oprah was amazed:

"We thought all those beepers were doctors! You're sitting in the theater and all those beepers are going off—and we thought they were all *doctors*!"

She was asked how she would like to have Robert De Niro as a leading man in a film she might make:

"I could take a few weeks *of this lifetime* and give it all up right now if I could do a movie with him!"

After a show about what rage and anger does to people, Oprah talked about the effects of her show on the audiences across the country:

"People are no different in Podunk than in Chicago. [Here] they may dress differently and live in high-rises, but when it comes to human desires and human hopes, we are all the same. One of the reasons I enjoy doing shows like today's is it lets people know they are not alone. Every woman who has felt that sense of rage inside will recognize herself by seeing the other women, and will hopefully get help."

On a show featuring prostitutes, Oprah asked one of them if she thought the oldest profession was respectable. One woman spoke up:

"Do I think it's a respectable profession? I think it's better than being a tramp." (FYI: A prostitute charges money; a "tramp" gives it away free.)

Life-in-Hollywood Department, during a discussion with Jackie Collins:

JACKIE: I've sat in a restaurant where there's three good tables, and somebody's been at the third table, and they've actually given the maître d' five hundred dollars to get shifted to the best table! Now *that* is kind of pushing it a little far.

OPRAH: Five hundred! No wonder my fifty doesn't work.

JACKIE: Well, some Hollywood husbands tip the maître d' with a little bag of cocaine.

OPRAH: Oh, my goodness.

The letters pour in to Oprah Winfrey every day—at least a hundred every twenty-four hours—and they prove one thing to her:

"Every one is more personal than the next. I mean, all of them are just incredibly, 'You're-the-last-person-I-have-to-turn-to' kind of letters. And yes, I suppose it's a responsibility, if you look at it that way. But we just look at it as another adjunct to the show. We don't do a show without offering [help] to people."

It's not only letters that Oprah attracts:

"I was walking down the street the other day, and a woman bus driver pulled her bus over, jumped off it, and ran down the street to shake my hand. The bus was full, and this was five o'clock traffic, but the passengers loved it. Everyone was clapping, and I said to myself, 'This is something! I must be somebody!' "

During a promotional tour from one city to the next just before her show was nationally syndicated, Oprah compared the day-to-day talking with being a politician in a political race:

"It's like campaigning. It's given me a greater respect for candidates and what they go through. I think they ought to win based on how many cities they went to, not how many votes they get."

Asked by one reporter during the same promo tour if she ever took a vacation, she laughed and shot back:

"Vacation? *This* is my vacation! I do movies on vacation. Oh, I may get around to a 'real' one in about 1997."

For a woman who never had a penny in her hand when she was small, and who grew up in the worst of poverty, Oprah Winfrey now has control of millions of dollars—all her own! Is she still that "spending fool" she once called herself?

> "I have allotted myself to personally only spend a million dollars this year [1986]. That's how much I'm giving myself to play with. I can do that without worrying if this ends, will I have enough to eat."

When she became a millionaire in 1986, Oprah discovered that she was spending every cent she made. Her manager instructed her to cut up her charge cards and the card she had for the bank cash machine. The idea was to pay for everything she bought with cash.

> "Before, if I couldn't decide which of two dresses I wanted, I bought them both. Now if I don't have the cash, I don't buy it. And when you have to count out five hundred dollars in bills—it makes you stop and think!"

Oprah has a philosophy about being generous and giving:

> "I'll give you the shirt off my back, as long as you don't ask for it."

Commenting about spending money and how money affects her:

> "Money just *falls* off me. I mean it *falls* off!"

She loves fur coats and has a closet full of them. But she also realizes that animal-lovers and some environmentalists don't *believe* in using animals to make coats. Her rejoinder:

> "I say minks were *born* to die!"

She has developed a philosophy of life through the years that has come from her early involvement with the church and with her experiences in life. Because of that, it is a bit secular, and a bit religious.

"I understand my commonality with the human experience. We all want to be happy, we have sad times. If you have lived, you have overeaten at one period or another. I'm not afraid to show those feelings. I can say, 'Look, I have been there, I understand how it feels to be in love with somebody and not have him love you back.' People say, 'Doggone that Oprah, isn't she something?' But they don't realize sometimes that I'm just like them."

How much like the character Sofia from *The Color Purple* is the real Oprah Winfrey?

"I have a hard time saying no to people. It comes from wanting to be liked, and I don't have the courage to be disliked yet. I hate confrontation; even if a person is an absolute asshole, I try to pacify him, make him feel good. I don't have it in me to be like Sofia."

On being observed jogging at Northwestern University's track near her downtown Chicago condominium, wearing a brilliant orange dress with a rhinestone-studded belt, Oprah observed:

"I'm glad to be doing the show from the Midwest. People here can still be shocked."

The hugging and kissing can be a problem:

"You notice people are starting to kiss me a lot lately? Well, I always turn and give them my cheek. You don't want to say, 'How about a hug instead?' "

On promotional tour to plug her nationally syndicated show, Oprah discussed these types of tours with a reporter:

"I'm always interviewing people on my show who are in the midst of these types of promotional tours. I'm used to asking the questions. The only time I've answered this many questions was during *The Color Pur-*

ple. We did forty-two interviews in one day. It's like going through therapy. I normally don't sit around and analyze what I do, where I am, and the path that got me here. Now I find myself talking about things I never wondered about before."

Is Oprah "secure" or "insecure"—according to the psychological meaning of the term?

"I'm very secure. That's misinterpreted as arrogance, but not by anyone who knows me. I only play by my rules. I'm ruled by my own inner voice."

An Oprah-ism about giving and getting:

"If you don't give something back when you get, you don't keep."

All about Oprah and Chicago:

"I become totally excited when I just think about Chicago. Because being here has meant the recognition for me that I received in other places, but it has meant more because of the kind of city Chicago is. I call it 'cosmopolitan country.' "

When Oprah visited San Francisco recently, she had this to say about the City by the Bay:

"I love this town! You can quote me on that. It's got such a great energy . . . its own vibes. It's a civilized New York. The people are great and friendly."

When people write nasty letters to Oprah, they are frequently shocked to be invited to lunch with her. She now has a monthly luncheon she spends with people who hate her.

"I started a monthly luncheon club for my hate viewers. I read all the mail and pick out twelve of the most hostile witches and I take them to lunch. The first time, I spent four hours talking to them. We drank fourteen bottles of champagne!"

About the whole social whirl, generally:

"For the most part, I like people. But my head hurts when I have to be in any situation where people are being phony. So if I can't be myself and take my shoes off when my feet hurt, then I'm not going to do very well."

After a group of very rich high-rolling bachelors had agreed on her show that they never expected to sleep with a woman on the first date, Oprah turned to the slickest-looking of them and batted her eyelashes:

"How about you, Jimmy James? You don't look like you say, 'Let's wait.' "

"On the show the other day, I said, right out of the blue, 'We're going to post a 900 number now for you to vote if you think, yes, I should get my nose done.' "

Oprah has often been accused of having a "fatalistic" outlook on life. She has also been accused of believing in the old classic concept of "carpe diem"—seizing the day and living life to the hilt. Well, in a few words, here is Oprah's total philosophy of life:

"I'm one of those people who lives for the moment. If you concern yourself with what's going to happen a year from now, or five years from now, you defuse the moment. Whatever comes, comes. For this time, I enjoy the ascent. I don't worry about anything except getting thinner thighs."

13
The Oprah Steamroller

February 1987 was time again for the television sweeps. For the uninitiated, three months of each year have been designated "key" months for the audience-rating services—November, February, and May. For that reason, television viewing during the days and nights of these three key months occasionally resembles a carnival of some kind—or at least something closely resembling a carnival.

Upon the final "ratings"—the numbers of viewers and households watching the shows as determined scientifically by both the Nielsen service and the Arbitron service—depend the advertising fees each network will be able to charge for its commercials in the following months. Thus, the Nielsen and Arbitron ratings are crucial in the final determination of the relative popularity of the network's various programs and help set its ad rates.

Because of the importance of the specific weeks involved in the sweeps—so-called because each rating service "sweeps" across all possible stations to determine the number of viewers watching each individual program—most shows try to put their best foot forward. Best foot, best face, best whatever.

As long ago as March 1986 Oprah Winfrey's main rival on the air—Phil Donahue—had been planning one of the most spectacular miniseries of talk-show programs yet on record. He and his people had been working for months—indeed, years—in an attempt to repeat his hugely successful "space bridge" broadcast of 1986.

"Space bridge" is satellite lingo. Donahue had initiated two so-called citizens' summits—conversations between people in Russia and America, between studio audiences in the Soviet Union and the United States. These were masterminded and initiated in the United States. Each program was co-moderated by Donahue and a Soviet journalist named Vladimir Pozner.

Telecast both in the Soviet Union and the United States, this space bridge was so much talked about that Donahue determined to repeat the concept—but with one vital difference. What Donahue dreamed of was to go to Russia and do the show there, then bring it back and broadcast it in the States.

Making the dream come true was not impossible, it developed, because of the presence now in the Kremlin of Mikhail Gorbachev. Gorbachev had declared a new policy in effect in the Soviet Union, and was determined to prove that it existed. Called *glasnost*—"openness"—it meant that tourists and visitors to Russia would be allowed a more uninhibited access to the average Soviet citizen than in the past.

It took months to straighten out all the political and diplomatic wrinkles that, if they did not already exist, soon developed. But finally, in January 1987, all the red tape was cut away and Donahue and his crew were flying to Russia to make appearances in the Soviet Union over a period of ten whole days.

Word was out. During the first key week of the February sweeps, Donahue would feature five segments of his talk show subtitled DONAHUE IN RUSSIA.

The programs would feature a number of wide-ranging subjects, including discussions about alcoholism, morality, infidelity, religion, family life, birth control, abortion, medical benefits, the war in Afghanistan, refuseniks, and so on.

In the Oprah Winfrey camp there was some consternation about what to do to counter this onslaught of ratings-rousing programming. Donahue had a built-in blockbuster that he would pit against Oprah during what broadcasters consider the most important week in the February sweeps, the first full week.

There were, of course, two possibilities in moving to counterattack. Oprah could opt out for the period and simply do her own thing as if Donahue's Russian invasion did not exist. After all, in most of her key cities she was ahead of him—and had been since September, when she went national. In effect, she would simply concede the week to Donahue.

Or she could try to mount some kind of spectacular ploy against Donahue—go for the jugular, so to speak.

Experts in history have often said that competition is the catalyst for some of the most marvelous changes in science, mathematics, and human sociology. That is, competition is the essential ingredient in the greatest advances of mankind.

In the world of show business, competition may not be quite so important, or so pronounced—but the analogy is certainly appropriate. Competition makes for some of the best shows on television—just because a superstar fears someone else may beat him or her out.

This was no exception.

In much the same manner that the opening week between Oprah and Donahue back in September 1986 had determined and set the style for the weeks to follow, so would this key week in February set the tone for the rivalry—and underline its interest.

What to do?

When Oprah opened against Donahue in September she had gone to her basic strength—women's problems. The specific theme used at the time was the problem of getting a man. But such strength can be a weakness when set against an international issue like Russian-American relations.

Donahue had a winner *in hand*. Well?

Oprah had her weaknesses as well as her strengths. One of the patent weaknesses that had been much promoted through the media by writers of all shades of the political and sociological spectrum was the fact that Oprah had never pretended to have a strong civil rights stance.

She *believed* in civil rights. She had even based her motion-picture role in *The Color Purple* on a known civil rights leader. But she was not one to mount the podium at the drop of a hat and blast out for the rights of blacks and other minorities.

And so—

Maybe this was the time to declare herself a card-carrier in the civil rights movement. Maybe this time she could honestly put her views in focus and tell her viewers how she felt.

Largely to focus media attention on the official commemoration of Martin Luther King, Jr.'s birthday on January 19, a group of civil rights demonstrators had decided to make an issue of Forsyth County, Georgia.

Unknown to most people in the country, Forsyth County is lily-white in its sociological structure. That is, there are no blacks or other minorities living within its geographical boundaries. It is one of those unbelievable anachronisms occasionally discovered in the Old South.

Consider: In the middle of the Deep South, here was a

large area of the countryside that did *not* have a black resident living in it!

The plan for the civil rights demonstrators, led by the Reverend Hosea L. Williams, was to focus media attention on this "stronghold" of Ku Klux Klanism and other types of racism—right here in Forsyth County!

The "gimmick" intrigued the media. Reporters, photographers, cameramen, and broadcasters appeared in some strength to watch the civil rights demonstration held on January 17, 1987, in Cumming, Georgia. Even if nothing happened, it would be a nice little sidebar for the evening news.

The people of Forsyth County reacted in predictable fashion. The members of several local racist groups, including members of the Ku Klux Klan, immediately announced a counterdemonstration. These counterdemonstrators would appear opposite the demonstrators to give the incursion into Forsyth County what they deemed to be the "proper balance."

By the time the civil rights group had formed, the counterdemonstrators were well in position, waving signs and shouting racist slogans. They held aloft Confederate flags. The signs read, in part:

WHITE CIVIL RIGHTS!
GO HOME NIGGER!

The civil rights demonstrators sang songs—"We Shall Overcome," among others.

Pretty soon what had been expected all along occurred. There was a spate of rock throwing.

Then it faded out and all the people went home.

The feature made the news in many cities. But once the shouting and the fist shaking and the flag waving was over, it was all laid to rest.

For exactly how long?

Seven days.

For, exactly one week later, on January 24, the Reverend Hosea Williams reappeared in Cumming, Georgia, this time with an expanded group of civil rights demonstrators. At this point the group numbered some twenty thousand. This was a number far in excess of the small band that had invaded Cumming the week before.

Now the counterdemonstrators were augmented to a similar degree by shouting and ranting men and women and children. During this second encounter, the confrontation was so unruly that the local police force under the direction of Sheriff Wesley C. Walraven, Jr., arrested sixty of the most vociferous and active counterdemonstrators.

The second confrontation, as might be expected, drew a greater degree of attention from the various media. This story was much bigger than the first. Howling, half-mad, racist hooligans were featured in most of the news coverage of the event that night.

Moderate people in Forsyth County immediately protested the *tone* of the news coverage. Many were unhappy that only the racists were shown. There *were* moderates in Forsyth County, it was pointed out. Many of them had participated—on the side of the civil rights groups—but this fact had gone unnoticed by the press.

Two weeks before the television sweeps commenced, this second "Cumming" story hit the media. It gave Oprah and *The Oprah Winfrey Show* food for thought: Would Oprah find it profitable to call in the leaders of the civil rights march, and the leaders of the counterdemonstration in Cumming, and let them confront one another?

Members of the audience could then participate in the discussion by confronting whoever they thought was wrong—or right.

Oprah was agreeable at first. She discussed the show with her producer, director, and crew. Then they all began thinking. Why hew to the formula? Sure, the Oprah Winfrey formula was a good one. You put the people on one side together, and you put the people on the other side together, and you played them like a game of point and counterpoint. The confrontation itself became the show, bringing in the viewers for a dramatic and exciting contest.

But maybe—

If Forsyth County was so lily-white—*why* was it lily-white? Oprah's researchers soon found out. It had to do with an event that had occurred back in 1912, at the beginning of the century! It was a dramatic enough story to provide an anchor for the show.

What if instead of flying the protagonists in to the Chicago studio, the show itself flew down to Georgia and broadcast the incursion of a black celebrity—Oprah Winfrey—right at the scene of the demonstrations?

Then Oprah would have firsthand knowledge of the place and of its people. She could feature *that* on her show. The cameras would show all there was to see. Everybody would have a chance to defend his or her position.

Half-black, half-white—that was the proposed scenario at first. But that would mean getting the blacks into the county with the least trouble possible. Certainly the police would cooperate. But—

Cooler heads prevailed. Having both sides equally represented in Cumming itself would create a terribly volatile and dangerous situation. The audience, being confined in a hermetically sealed place, would create a potentially explosive situation.

"People would have chosen sides, and that would be *it,*" Oprah decided. No. It would *not* work. It was too dangerous.

Then the idea of a "conversation" surfaced. The theme of the show would be not a confrontation, but an attempt to "understand." The audience could be limited to members of Forsyth County. They would simply tell their story to Oprah—both sides of it.

Thus the show itself would provide an attempt at understanding the feelings and motivations of the people of all-white Forsyth County and to learn why this community had not allowed black people to live in it since 1912.

Setting up the scene for the show itself was not all that easy. There were no public facilities that seemed adequate for the number of people in a typical Oprah audience. Finally a small restaurant—the Dinner Deck—was selected. There was enough room there for the television crew to set themselves up and put down chairs for the people who would make up the audience.

When news of the upcoming show hit the press there was sudden and jarring dissonance in the air—produced by civil rights activists and their friends. It was immediately obvious to them that the audience would be slanted in one direction—away from them.

Where were the minorities in the audience? Who would represent them? How could the show be objective if only one side was represented?

But there was no pulling back now. Oprah was getting good play in the press. She was creating built-in interest in the Monday show—which would go up against the first day of Donahue's fantastically ratings-rich Russian visit.

Oprah Winfrey did not back down.

The Oprah Blockbuster

When the show began that Monday in Cumming's Dinner Deck restaurant, with residents of Forsyth County present in the audience, the Reverend Hosea Williams appeared outside in the street, protesting the fact that there were no blacks in the audience to present the civil rights side of the question.

Despite learning of his presence outside at the beginning of the show, Oprah told the audience: "We are here simply to ask why Forsyth County has not allowed black people to live here in seventy-five years." She did not mention Mr. Williams but confined her statement to the theme of the show.

Even with the audience limited to people who lived in Forsyth County, it was not the easiest group in the world to handle. When Oprah set the tone of the show by asking the question, the story slowly came out, told by members of the audience.

In the year 1912, a white woman named Mary Crow was said to have been raped by three black men. On September 8, 1912, the three were lynched. On September 23, the word went out that all blacks would be "out" of the county.

From that point on, there had simply been no blacks welcomed in Forsyth County.

"They have the right to live wherever they want to," one woman in the audience said. "But we have the right to have a white community too."

This was too much for Oprah, who usually kept her civil rights opinions to herself. "I like the way you speak of *them*. It's like, you know, black people come from Mars or something."

Later on, when a man in the audience insisted that "Forsyth County is a nice place to live, a nice county," Oprah was heard to murmur into the mike, "Yeah. For white people."

The most vociferous racist in the group was Frank Shirley, a member of the Committee to Keep Forsyth County White. He said that most of the civil rights marchers who had come into Cumming for the demonstrations in January were "Communists and homosexuals." He said that many members of the demonstration were "dupes of the Communists." He had even seen two planeloads of "guys from San Francisco" fly into town. The implication was obvious.

According to Shirley, the throwing of rocks and other demonstrations against blacks—the waving of Confederate flags and the hurling of epithets against "niggers"—was "the largest white people's protest against Communism in the last thirty years."

Most of the members of the audience were not quite so afflicted with tunnel vision. They were unhappy over the media treatment of their community.

"There are people who would throw rocks," one woman admitted, "but the majority of our people are not like that at all."

Another in the audience said that it was unfair to judge the entire county on the attitudes of a minority of residents.

Still another woman said that she herself had participated in the demonstrations, but had not been on the side of the rock throwers and hate-mongers. She had marched with the civil rights people.

"I felt it was important for Forsyth Countians to be there and to make it clear that we welcome all law-abiding people in our community."

Another said that the jeering and the rock throwing from the whites "really makes you feel ashamed."

It made for exciting television theater.

Los Angeles Times columnist Howard Rosenberg, who reviewed the show later, called it one of the best talk shows he had seen in some time.

"Yes, the show was self-serving, just as the news media always exploit the problems of others for a good story. Yes, Winfrey knew that showing her black face against a sea of Forsyth County whites promised blockbuster ratings. But that didn't invalidate the premise of the show.

"Winfrey was a one-woman ambassador, surely the most curious Southern belle many whites inside the restaurant had ever seen. TV talk shows can't really destroy prejudice, but in this hour, at least, the good guys got the last word."

In addition, "The show had everything: spontaneity, drama, conflict, tension, peril, anger, and honesty. Emotions were high and raw. Forsyth County's record of barring black residents is no fantasy. Yet the vast majority in the room preached racial harmony, and only a minority —only a handful of Klan, Nazis, and other white supremacists present—spread hatred."

The show was "great TV and great Oprah."

The Donahue Blockbuster

The *Donahue* show pitted against the Oprah show could have been coming from New York or from Chicago or from any other place in the United States. But nevertheless it was indeed coming from Moscow. The only telltale difference lay in the fact that each of the members of the audience was wired with earphones to provide simultaneous translations.

Monday's program examined Russian family life. It was obvious that Donahue was toning down his general delivery in order not to confuse and anger the Soviets.

Even with Donahue's ability to rouse people, he had a heavy time of it getting the question-and-answer session on the rails. The people simply weren't going to talk about what he wanted them to talk about.

He asked them first of all what their opinions were on birth control and abortion. The response was a kind of unbelieving silence. It didn't get much better when he moved on to Soviet morality—especially sexual morality.

Donahue was determined to get *something* out of them. He asked the audience if there was the same double standard in Russia that there was in the United States: that is, if a man fooled around outside the marriage it was all right, but if a woman did, it was not.

The Soviets seemed stunned at the idea. Well anyway, stunned at the idea that such a subject could be discussed on the air! Several individuals tried to answer his question. But there was no really conclusive answer.

The talk moved on to the number of children most

people believed in having in the Soviet Union. From that it wandered into housing conditions. Because of the fairly small apartments, families did not grow so swiftly as in America.

Then the discussion settled on child rearing. The Soviets made it clear they wanted to teach their children to be able to get along in life, to solve their own problems. Of course, the most important thing for a Russian parent was to teach the children not to be materialistic.

Mostly the Soviets were interested in Donahue's reaction to Russia and the Russian people. "How do you like it here, Phil?" one woman asked with a beaming smile.

Donahue said he was "very, very impressed by the compassion, generosity, and friendliness of your people." He said that the Soviet and American people needed to "reach out" more to one another.

Tuesday's program involved a roomful of Soviet teenagers, who listened first to a rock band and then began talking. Once again, Donahue had trouble getting them going.

"You are like sheep!" he exploded at one point. "Are we going to spend the entire program listening to you tell how wonderful everything is here?"

One of the members of the audience stood up. "What can we do if everything here is all right? Do you want us to create problems?"

During this session Donahue was dressed in a red sweater and blue jeans, with his tie loosened and pulled away from his throat. He finally steered them into a discussion of sex.

"You had sex when you were eighteen years old?" Donahue repeated after one statement. "Did you use a contraceptive?"

The young man said he had done so.

"Are most Soviet boys like you—conscientious?" Donahue asked.

The young man said they were.

Donahue turned to God. "Most Americans think Russians are discouraged from believing in God. But this is perhaps a stereotype."

Several answered him. It was not that they were "discouraged from believing in God." It was more that science had proved that God did not exist. But that did not matter. The real question was not God or His existence, but—you guessed it!—the "materialism" of American culture.

Most Russians loved the American people, one of the members of the audience said. "Americans are closest to the Soviet people in spirit."

Donahue said that Americans were worried about the Soviet Union's policy of expansion. "It is the belief of some Americans that you do this by military might," Donahue said in his lecture-platform diction. "However, the vast majority of people in the United States admire you."

The young people in Russia said that they understood Americans. "We know a lot about you," one young woman told Donahue. "The arms race is in response to you."

Yet one student who was about to go into the army promised: "I guarantee to you that I will not invade your country."

Another student admitted that he would not want to fight in Afghanistan. "I'm ready to die for my homeland; I'm not ready to die for others."

However, if he was called on to fight for Russia in Afghanistan, he told Donahue he would do it. Why? It was his "duty."

There were cheers.

Another youth pointed out that all United States military was dictated by the "military-industrial complex."

Donahue responded quickly: "You have just as narrow a vision of us, if you hold that view, as you accuse us of having of you."

Oprah's Blockbuster II

On Tuesday, while Donahue was talking to Russian teenagers, Oprah was doing a typical "Oprah." This time she was interviewing a group of female impersonators who worked the night spots in Chicago.

One of these men in drag, with the unlikely name of "Chili" Pepper, made the statement of the day:

"Call me a bionic woman."

They called female impersonation a "craft"—a true art form. Of course, the whole idea of males dressed up as females dated back to Shakespearean days—even back to the Greek theater—when men were the only performers allowed onstage.

The males on Oprah's show were decked out in very expensive costumes. Oprah called attention to the jewelry and the clothes they wore in their roles as women.

"You must not do too badly in that kind of job," she said.

One of the impersonators conceded that it was indeed a pretty good gig.

Oprah asked one of the performers what happened when another male, not knowing this "female" was male, became interested in him/her. Talk got around to kissing and that kind of thing.

The performer said he/she had a rule. "I don't kiss people because I don't know where they've been."

That drew a smile from Oprah, who expanded the thought into an Oprah-ism: "I don't kiss you because I don't know where you've been, and you don't kiss me because you don't know where I've been!"

On Wednesday, Oprah countered "Donahue in Russia III" with a group of battered women who talked about their pasts. This was a hair-raising performance by the guests.

On Thursday, the subject was dieting, and on Friday, leather and lingerie.

Donahue visited Chernobyl on Thursday, and wound up the week with a show broadcast from New York, with Soviet journalists, and Vladimir Pozner as anchorperson.

It was quite a performance.

All in all, it was that first show that set the proper tone for Oprah's success over the week-long haul. In New York, which was a crucial viewing area for Oprah, sweeps week went hands-down to Oprah, in spite of Donahue's highly publicized trip to Russia and the large number of New Yorkers who would be interested in his show because of past loyalties.

According to the Nielsen ratings for the week, Oprah rang in at 11.0, with Donahue at 7.1. Arbitron had Oprah a 9.7 to Donahue's 4.8. The rating, incidentally, represented the percentage of New York's television-equipped homes tuned in to the program.

It was a clear-cut victory for Oprah.

And there were other victories in store for her.

Along about this time *TV Guide* came up with a general review of *The Oprah Winfrey Show* by Don Merrill. It was the next thing to a rave.

"If you haven't yet treated yourself to *The Oprah Winfrey Show,*" he wrote, "we suggest that you do so soon. The woman's warmth alone makes her a natural for television and that, along with her ability to deal with serious or trivial subject matter with equal skill, results in a remarkably satisfying talk show."

What made the show work, Merrill said, was the fact that "beneath a homey personality that invites confidences, there is a confident, talented journalist digging for truth. And members of her audience sometimes get so caught up with the subject that they blurt out sensitive secrets."

There was no set formula on the matters covered, he wrote. "Sexual subjects are a staple, of course, but Winfrey is not preoccupied with the subject. She is more inclined to treat unusual subjects and she has more than a touch of show biz in her."

He wound up with the comment that "She deserves every bit of her success."

Meanwhile, a lot of television and movie projects were being put into the works for Oprah by her attorney-manager Jeffrey Jacobs through Harpo Productions.

One of these was a miniseries for television based on Gloria Naylor's novel *The Women of Brewster Place,* about the trials and tribulations of a group of black women living in a ghetto area.

Oprah was hoping to feature her actress friends Alfre Woodward, Phylicia Rashad (Bill Cosby's "wife" on his super-successful weekly sitcom series), and *Fame* star Debbie Allen (Phylicia's sister).

In addition to that project, Oprah was being wooed by Reeves Entertainment to do a weekly half-hour television sitcom herself, featuring her as—wouldn't you know?—a talk-show hostess on television!

This show would be produced by ABC-TV in association with King World and Reeves Entertainment. The problem that came up was an obvious one: Would she be able to do all this and carry on with her own show besides?

An aide on *The Oprah Winfrey Show* cleared that up. "She's free to leave the show as soon as it finishes taping at ten in the morning. You'd be surprised at how much she can accomplish during a week's time."

"Right now I make a lot of money," Oprah told a reporter for *Adweek,* "and you can only buy so many towels and so many houses. . . . Money is not the issue. The purpose of [Harpo Productions] is to invest in projects that we think are worthwhile."

She said that she would like to do something more challenging than the "black or fat" roles she was being routinely offered. With one exception:

"I'd like to do Dinah Washington—a great, great blues singer who had several different husbands and used to sexually exhaust her men."

Oprah does not have several husbands—does not actually have even one—nor does she sing professionally. Whether or not she would exhaust any men she had is largely unknown. But she would certainly like to play the part.

In *Parade* magazine recently, Lloyd Shearer questioned the exact size of Oprah Winfrey's personal "fortune." He disputed several statements quoted from King World about the amount of money she would make in 1987, and questioned the fact that she had been paid, as was said, $1 million for each of her acting jobs in the films *The Color Purple* and *Native Son*.

Although claiming that "estimates of her fortune are highly exaggerated," he wound up with a sudden about-face admission that, after all, what she did have and would get was considerable.

"Not bad," as he wrote, "for a girl who was born into rural poverty of sorts in Kosciusko, Mississippi."

A case of praising with faint damnation. To echo Shearer's admission—no, not bad at all!

Bibliography

Magazine Articles

Allis, Tim. "You Could Feel the Chill in the Hair." *People,* September 22, 1986.

———. "Does She Have a Sister Named Ohcuorg?" *People,* February 18, 1987.

Andersen, Chris. "Meet Oprah Winfrey." *Good Housekeeping,* August 1986.

Ansen, David. "We Shall Overcome." *Newsweek,* December 30, 1985.

Barthel, Joan. "Here Comes Oprah!" *Ms.,* August 1986.

Bednarski, P. J. "The Talk Show Diva Named Oprah." *Channels of Communication,* January/February 1986.

"Blacks on Television; On a Screen, Darkly." *The Economist,* May 17, 1986.

Blake, Richard A. "Survivors." *America,* February 1, 1986.

Brock, Fran. "Oprah Goes National: Chicago TV Star Celebrates Syndication at Outdoor Bash." *Adweek,* September 15, 1986.

Class, Kelly. "The Top-Selling Products, Region by Region: Fear of Baldness; The Midwest." *Adweek,* November 4, 1985.

Dempsey, John. "Winfrey's Whammo Syndie Deal." *Variety,* December 31, 1986.

Edwards, Audrey. "Stealing the Show." *Essence,* October 1986.

"Goldberg, Avery, Winfrey, up for Oscars in 'Purple.' " *Jet,* February 24, 1986.

Goldfarb, Susan. "I Drove the Devil out of Oprah Winfrey—Says Her Dad." *Globe,* March 3, 1987.

Grossberger, Lewis. "Can We Not Talk?" *Rolling Stone,* December 4, 1986.

Hey, Kenneth R. "The Color Purple." *USA Today,* March 1986.

"Jgr." "The Color Purple (Review)." *Variety,* December 18, 1985.

Johnson, Pamela. "Fine Tuning!" *Essence,* July 1985.

Kael, Pauline. "Sacred Monsters." *The New Yorker,* December 30, 1985.

Kauffmann, Stanley. "Signs of the Times." *The New Republic,* January 27, 1986.

Krauthammer, Charles. "Celebrities in Politics: A Cure." *Time,* April 21, 1986.

Lyons, Judith F. "That's Show Business." *Time,* April 28, 1986.

McIver, Mary, ed. "People." *Maclean's,* May 5, 1986.

Markey, Judy. "Brassy, Sassy Oprah Winfrey." *Cosmopolitan,* September 1986.

Merrill, Don. "The Oprah Winfrey Show (Review)." *TV Guide,* February 14, 1987.

Millander, Lucius. "Riding the Ratings." *Black Enterprise,* January 1986.

"Mor." "The Oprah Winfrey Show (Review)." *Variety,* March 12, 1986.

Neill, Michael. "That's Okay, They've Got Fat Heads." *Time,* June 2, 1986.

Neisser, Judith. "Grand Oprah." *United,* December 1986.

Nelson, Jill. "The Man Who Saved Oprah Winfrey." *Washington Post Magazine,* December 14, 1986.

Noel, Pamela. "Lights! Camera! Oprah!" *Ebony,* April 1985.

"NOW Honors Oprah Winfrey for 'Color Purple' Role." *Jet,* June 30, 1986.

"Oprah Heads South." *Newsweek,* February 28, 1987.

"Oprah Winfrey, Talk-Show Hostess/Actress." *New Woman,* March 1987.

"Q.A." *Parade,* December 14, 1986.

Rautbord, Sugar. "Oprah Winfrey." *Interview,* March 1986.

Richman, Alan. "Oprah." *People,* January 12, 1987.

R.Z. "Winfrey Rivals Cosby as Top TV Wage Earner." *TV Guide,* January 17, 1987.

Sanders, Richard, reported by Barbara Kleban Mills. "TV Host Oprah Winfrey, Chicago's Biggest Kick, Boots up for a Star-Making Role in The Color Purple." *People,* December 16, 1985.

Schine, Cathleen. "Oprah Winfrey: She Believes." *Vogue,* May 1986.

Seitz, Michael H. "Pop Purple." *The Progressive,* February 1986.

Shearer, Lloyd. "Oprah Winfrey—How Rich?" *Parade,* February 15, 1987.

Smith, R. C. "She Once Trashed Her Apartment to Make a Point." *TV Guide,* August 30, 1986.
"Tenuous Places." *Commonweal,* January 31, 1986.
Tornabene, Lyn. "Here's Oprah." *Woman's Day,* October 1, 1986.
Turner, Richard. "Winfrey Discussing Comedy Series with ABC." *TV Guide,* February 28, 1987.
"TV's Hall of Flukey Fame." *People,* August 25, 1986.
Waldron, Robert. "Oprah Winfrey: My Guy." *Star,* January 13, 1987.
Waters, Harry F., with Patricia King. "Chicago's Grand New Oprah." *Newsweek,* December 31, 1984.
Zaslow, Jeffrey. "Against the Odds: Morning Star." *Savvy,* September 1986.
Zehme, Bill. "It Came from Chicago." *Spy,* December 1986.
Zoglin, Richard, reported by Cathy Booth (New York) and Jack E. White (Chicago). " 'People Sense the Realness.' " *Time,* September 15, 1986.
———, reported by James O. Jackson (Moscow) and William Tynan (New York). "Stirring up the Comrades." *Time,* February 16, 1987.

Newspaper Articles

Anderson, Jon. "Wingin' It with Channel 7's Oprah Winfrey." *Chicago Tribune,* March 13, 1984.
———. "Stations Schedule 'Refinement' in '85." *Chicago Tribune,* January 1, 1985.
———. "Oprah Winfrey Conquers 'Tonight Show' Challenger." *Chicago Tribune,* January 31, 1985.
Attanasio, Paul. " 'Purple,' 'Africa' Top Oscar List." *The Washington Post,* February 6, 1986.
———. "The Odds and the Oscars." *The Washington Post,* March 23, 1986.
———. "The Film Calendar." *The Washington Post,* September 7, 1986.
Barnum, Art. "Coretta Scott King Urges Campaign to End Hunger." *Chicago Tribune,* January 21, 1985.
Bayles, Martha. "Oprah vs. Phil: Warmth Wins Out." *The Wall Street Journal,* January 26, 1987.
Benson, Sheila. "Two Women of Substance in Unlikely Settings: 'The Color Purple.' " *Los Angeles Times,* December 18, 1985.
Borden, Jeff. "Oprah!" *Charlotte Observer,* September 6, 1986.
Brooke, Jill. "Winfrey's True-to-Life Sitcom." N.Y. *Daily News,* February 20, 1987.
Buck, Jerry. "America Will Soon See All That Oprah Winfrey Has Got." *Associated Press,* August 23, 1986.

Carmody, John. "The TV Column." *The Washington Post,* February 24, 1986; May 20, 1986; July 7, 1986; August 1, 1986; August 26, 1986; September 18, 1986; October 17, 1986; October 21, 1986.

Carter, Bill. "Oprah Winfrey: Still the Talk of the Town." *Baltimore Sun,* September 9, 1986.

Clegg, Legrand H., II. "Bad Black Roles in 'Purple.' " ("Calendar.") *Los Angeles Times,* February 16, 1986.

" 'The Color Purple': Spielberg, Syrupy, and Slow-Moving." *The Washington Post,* December 20, 1985.

Conconi, Chuck. "Personalities." *The Washington Post,* February 10, 1986; March 10, 1986.

Corry, John. "A Week of 'Donahue' Taped in Soviet Union." *The New York Times,* February 9, 1987.

Dawidziak, Mark. "Spontaneity Is Key for TV Hostess." *Akron Beacon Journal,* August 3, 1986.

"Different Kind of Talk Show for Oprah." *Chicago Tribune,* January 10, 1985.

Dorsey, Tom. "Breezy and Outrageous Oprah Winfrey Offers Distinct Talk-Show Choice." *Louisville Courier-Journal,* September 8, 1986.

Duffy, Mike. "Is Detroit Ready for Oprah Show?" *Detroit Free Press,* August 31, 1986.

Fetherston, Drew. "Oprah Winfrey Has Arrived." *Newsday,* September 8, 1986.

"Forsyth Whites Tell Oprah Why." N.Y. *Daily News,* February 10, 1987.

Gardella, Kay. "Getting to Know U.S.S.R.: Donahue Shows Aim to Thaw Cold War." N.Y. *Daily News,* February 9, 1987.

Gilliam, Dorothy. "The Show Should Go On." *The Washington Post,* April 28, 1986.

Gelb, Lisa Serene. "Personalities." *The Washington Post,* April 5, 1986.

Harmetz, Aljean. "Learning to Live with Runaway Fame." *The New York Times,* May 18, 1986.

"How Oprah Winfrey Got Her Name." *Star,* February 17, 1987.

Howe, Desson. "Purple Power." *The Washington Post,* December 19, 1985.

———. "Just One for My Son." *The Washington Post,* January 26, 1986.

———. "Partying over Politics." *The Washington Post,* October 6, 1986.

Kastor, Elizabeth. "Ringing in the Newlyweds." *The Washington Post,* April 28, 1986.

Kempley, Rita. "Tinseltown's Rush—From Streep to Spies." *The Washington Post,* November 29, 1985.

———. " 'Purple': Making Whoopi a Star." *The Washington Post,* December 20, 1985.

Lavin, Cheryl. "It's All Going Oprah's Way." *Chicago Tribune,* December 19, 1985.

Levey, Bob. "Washington." *The Washington Post,* October 2, 1986.

Maginnis, Amy. "Oprah Winfrey: Taking Control of Her Own Life." *The Daily Republic* (Fairfield, Calif.), August 10, 1986.

Maksian, George. "It's High Noon at 4 p.m." N.Y. *Daily News,* December 15, 1986.

———. "TV." N.Y. *Daily News,* February 24, 1987.

Mann, Bill. "Oprah Winfrey: A Refreshingly Different TV Host." *Oakland Tribune,* September 8, 1986.

Mansfield, Stephanie. "And Now, Heeeere's Oprah!" *The Washington Post,* October 21, 1986.

———. "The Really Big Story." *The Washington Post,* February 27, 1986.

Margulies, Lee. "Winfrey, KTLA Comedies Stir up a Ratings Storm." *Los Angeles Times,* October 3, 1986.

Maslin, Janet. "Film: 'The Color Purple,' from Steven Spielberg." *The New York Times,* December 18, 1985.

Mathews, Jack. "Three 'Color Purple' Actresses Talk about Its Impact." *Los Angeles Times,* January 31, 1986.

Michaelson, Judith. "Richard Wright's 'Native Son' Finds Its Spot in Show-Biz Sun." *Los Angeles Times,* May 1, 1986.

———. "Seeking 'Native Son' Hollywood Tackles Richard Wright's 1940 Novel." *Los Angeles Times,* May 11, 1986.

Milloy, Courtland. "On Seeing 'The Color Purple.'" *The Washington Post,* February 18, 1986.

———. "Local Affairs Television Is Taking a Beating Here." *The Washington Post,* June 24, 1986.

Mills, David. "TV Hostess Goes National with Humor and 'Reality.'" *Washington Times,* September 9, 1986.

Mitchard, Jacquelyn. "Ex-Milwaukeean a New Darling of TV." *Milwaukee Journal,* February 10, 1985.

Morago, G. Phillip. "Winfrey Cheered at UConn" *Hartford Courant,* February 23, 1987.

Morgan, Thomas. "Troubled Girl's Evolution into an Oscar Nominee." *The New York Times,* March 4, 1986.

Mueller, Roxanne T. "Here's . . . Oprah!" Cleveland *Plain Dealer,* August 10, 1986.

Mulligan, Moira. "Personalities." *The Washington Post,* August 12, 1986.

Novit, Mel. "Outspoken Oprah Spins TV Talk into Gold." *Kansas City Times,* August 22, 1986.

Oldenburg, Don. "Career File." *The Washington Post,* May 28, 1986.

"Oprah Winfrey: A Good Neighbor to Invite for a Chat." *Newsday,* September 10, 1986.

Payne, Les. "Oprah and Phil in Million-Dollar TV Fight." *Stamford Advocate,* January 19, 1987.

Radcliffe, Donnie. "Talk Shows Drop Patti Davis." *The Washington Post,* March 12, 1986.

"Rights Leader Arrested in Georgia." *The New York Times,* February 10, 1987.

Robertson, Nan. "Actresses' Varied Roads to 'The Color Purple.' " *The New York Times,* February 13, 1986.

Rosenberg, Howard. "Winfrey Zeroing in on Donahue." *Los Angeles Times,* September 12, 1986.

———. "Donahue Wins All but the Refusenik Round." *Los Angeles Times,* February 4, 1987.

———. "Oprah's Sweep through Georgia." *Los Angeles Times,* February 16, 1987.

Rothenberg, Fred. "Oprah Leads the WABC Steamroller." N.Y. *Daily News,* February 19, 1987.

Scarupa, Henry. "Oprah Is Back." *Baltimore Sun,* September 8, 1986.

Shipp, E. R. "Blacks in Heated Debate over 'The Color Purple.' " *The New York Times,* January 27, 1986.

———. "Accent Is on Politics at Birthday Party in Chicago." *The New York Times,* April 17, 1986.

Sonsky, Steve. "Her TV Talk Show Hits People in the Heart." *Miami Herald,* September 7, 1986.

Sterritt, David. "Spielberg Scrubs and Softens 'The Color Purple.' " *The Christian Science Monitor,* December 20, 1985.

Stevens, Linda. "Blacks Busted at All-White Oprah Show." *New York Post,* February 10, 1987.

Thym, Jolene. "Oprah Fever to Hit Bay Area." *Daily Review* (Hayward, Calif.), August 11, 1986.

Trescott, Jacqueline. "Passions over 'Purple': Anger and Unease over Film's Depiction of Black Men." *The Washington Post,* February 5, 1986.

"Winfrey Brings Show to All-White Georgia County." *Stamford Advocate,* February 11, 1987.

Yorke, Jeffrey. "Film Talk." *The Washington Post,* December 13, 1985.

Young, Luther. "Oprah!" *Baltimore Sun,* January 27, 1985.

Zaslow, Jeffrey. "Chicago's Oprah Winfrey to Go National with Sassy TV Talk Show." *The Wall Street Journal,* March 7, 1986.

ABOUT THE AUTHOR

Norman King is the author of best-selling biographies of Erma Bombeck and Dan Rather. One of the best-known and most highly respected advertising executives in America, Mr. King is chairman of the American Marketing Complex, Inc., a major New York investment and media company. He is considered the dean of barter advertising in America.